P9-EAO-149

Creating Contagious Leadership

*9 Habits that Inspire
a Leadership Culture*

By John Hersey

Creating Contagious Leadership

Copyright ©2003
by John Hersey

All rights reserved. No portion of this publication may be reproduced,
stored in a retrieval system, or transmitted, in any form or by any means,
electronic, mechanical, photocopying, recording, or otherwise, without
the prior written permission of the copyright owner.

Leaders Publishing Group

Library of Congress Number 2003113392

ISBN: 0-9745593-0-X

Printed in the United States of America

10 9 8 7 6 5

Foreword

Managers manage a process. Leaders inspire and grow people. Managers *tell*. Leaders *influence*. Managers often focus on the *process*. Leaders always focus on the *person*.

Leaders make things happen. They guide people and motivate organizations. Transformational leaders impact who we are and what we do. They nurture our hearts and nourish our minds. We follow them not because we have to, but because we want to. We work harder and smarter not because they tell us to, but because they set the example for us.

Effective leaders know how to challenge, recognize, hire, develop and retain winners. They communicate and connect with their teams in substantially productive and purposeful ways. They dwell on "how we will" instead of "why we can't."

Transformational leadership is contagious and that's the premise of this book. John Hersey knows his stuff. He understands leadership from the inside out. He knows what works, what doesn't, and why. And in this wonderful book, he unveils the strategies and systems to help organizations create an environment where every person, regardless of position or title, can step up to the noble traits of leadership.

For over 30 years, Hersey has been building and leading teams in advertising, marketing, banking and several entrepreneurial ventures. He has been a practitioner of Contagious Leadership and a master producer of successful results.

A cum laude graduate from the Whittemore School of Business & Economics at the University of New Hampshire, John Hersey has educated many groups and trained many organizations to ensure leadership circles that increase productivity, enhance performance and generate profitability. He has "walked the talk" and has been in the trenches of business and industry. He's remarkably qualified to teach us all about leadership.

So, while managers may change their subordinates' behaviors, leaders really know how to change their employees' minds! A healthy mindset precedes positive behaviors. If you agree with this, you'll love this book. Written in an easy-to-read format and style, it's loaded with practical and pragmatic insight and advice.

Nido R. Qubein
Chairman, Great Harvest Bread Company

To Beverly, for giving me the greatest gift of love:
seeing beyond who I was to who I could be
and always standing for my greatness.

Acknowledgments

This book has taken 54 years to research, two weekends to write, and two years to muster the nerve to share it with, and request feedback from, several people I trust. To think for a moment that any of this could have happened alone would be the height of unabashed arrogance.

Without Beverly Belury — my best friend, business partner, biggest fan, strongest critic, soul mate and wife, *Creating Contagious Leadership* would still be an ambitious dream. She deserves a whole lot of credit from two points of view. First, as my partner, Beverly's strategic and creative thinking and input has consistently pushed the content of my speaking programs and workshops to higher levels. Her willingness to brainstorm market conditions, needs and solutions has helped us maintain a rigid focus on adding value to our clients.

Second, her encouragement, focus and enthusiasm gave me the inner strength to pursue my dream of starting John Hersey International. She has always supported my belief that I had something to contribute. And whenever I began to doubt my abilities, she was right there with a heavy dose of positive reinforcement, as well as an ample serving of energy and determination. Beverly has always been able to visualize our lives and our businesses with an endless supply of possibility. She has seen things in me that I was unable or unwilling to see. I will never be able to properly show my love or appreciation for her extraordinary presence in my life.

A special acknowledgement must also go to Nido Qubein and Steve Chandler. They were the first two people to read the full-length unedited manuscript of this book. It had been sitting quietly in my computer for over a year. Beverly insisted I share it with them because both are friends whose input we greatly admire. They were enthusiastic about this project, believing strongly that *Creating Contagious Leadership* was a message that needed to be shared. Their encouraging words and wonderful suggestions along the way have contributed greatly to the final product.

Over the past few years, I have been blessed to work with some wonderful clients. Each embraces the qualities and habits of Contagious Leadership and has asked me to help them move forward with a Contagious Leadership environment in their organization. I would be remiss if I did not acknowledge their contributions to me personally and to this book. From Wells Fargo Home Mortgage, there are more people to acknowledge than we have space to do so. In particular, I thank Tim Disbrow, Rich Land, Kim Castiglioni, Charlie Gerding, Jim Stavenger, Marie Imanaka, Chuck Current and Sherry Carey for believing in this work and allowing me to work closely with their people to create an environment of Contagious Leadership. The same is true for Jill Bellaus, Meenal Meehta and Pat Lambrecht of TAP Pharmaceuticals; Mario DiBlasi of CIGNA; Joe Bourdow of Valpack; Dianna Ruddick of Mass Mutual; Bill Conwell of Essex Technologies; Kelli Stiles of The Hartford; and Stephanie Trotter of GlaxoSmithKlein.

A word of gratitude must also go to all my friends and acquaintances in National Speakers Association, particularly the Arizona chapter. Never before have I been associated with a more talented and successful group of individuals who were as willing to share and support the success of others.

Thanks to Gayle Smart of James and Brookfield Publishers. She made the process of getting this book from manuscript to finished product a thoroughly enjoyable one; to Tim Peterson for his always-outstanding creative work on the cover design; and a special thanks to Kay duPont, our editor, for helping to make the manuscript into a vastly better book.

Introduction

The notion of helping organizations create Contagious Leadership first came to me in 1975, shortly after graduating from college and joining a $100 million bank in Massachusetts as a trainee. The size of the bank was not important; it was the culture that really intrigued me. This was an organization where everyone seemed to have a title. There were layers upon layers of titles, but little or no leadership. Everyone seemed to be waiting for someone else to lead. The employees waited for the supervisors, the supervisors waited for the officers and branch managers, the officers and branch managers waited for the assistant vice presidents, the assistant vice presidents waited for the vice presidents, who waited for the executive vice president who waited for the president. To me, the fresh-out-of-college smart 'aleck,' it appeared as though the bank was on autopilot, running itself. I do not mean that the leadership was bad. I mean that it did not exist. I couldn't identify a single person anywhere in the organization who was leading anyone anywhere.

Now, this was 1975 and the economy in Massachusetts was not strong. I was very happy to have this job, and happy to be learning and growing every day. Nevertheless, I began to think that work in general, and this job in particular, would be more fun, and probably more productive, if everyone in the organization stopped waiting for someone else to drive the bus. I began to wonder what it would be like to work in an organization where everyone took full responsibility for their jobs — not the lowest common denominator version of their jobs either, but the playing-full-out-version. The thought of this moved me to wonder what it would take to create an environment where everyone was excited, committed, positive, self-motivated and willing to think in terms of how to overcome challenges and serve customers rather than why they could not.

This was my first job. I had gotten a late start in college and was older than most college grads. But I was still young enough to think the grass might be greener in a larger organization or in a field other than banking. Time, maturity and experience would prove me very wrong. I spent seven years in banking and worked in organizations ranging in size from $100 million to over $1 billion in assets. It was rare to find anyone playing full-out, and rarer still to find employees at any level who were truly engaged and excited about their jobs. In the early 1980s, I moved to the advertising business. For the next 10 years I worked in one of the larger advertising agencies in the country. I worked with a varied list of clients — mostly large Fortune 1000 national or multinational organizations in retail, financial services, footwear, household products, manufacturing and hi-tech. Although the business was exciting, fast-paced, and loads of fun, it was more of the same in terms of leadership. In some organizations, people worked longer hours or at a faster pace, but the cultures were not all that different. Leadership was still a function of position and title, and people were still waiting for someone else to lead.

Please don't misunderstand. These were wonderful companies, with great brand names and terrific people. I am not at all being critical. But leadership was different then. In many organizations, there was one leader, or perhaps two or three. It was the person at the top, or the department heads and division executives. The focus was on managing the numbers, the systems and the process.

It has been nearly 30 years since I first began thinking about creating an environment of Contagious Leadership. I have made it my business to observe leaders, stay current on leadership trends, and form my own observations on the subject, and I came to three conclusions that greatly influenced me to write this book.

First, the subject of leadership, although relatively simple in its essence, has become altogether too complicated. It is not just that everyone seems to have an opinion, myself included, it is that many of the opinions about what it takes to be a leader are so detailed and complicated that we have to think too much. There are books galore. Academics, business executives, speakers, sports celebrities, coaches, entertainers, and community leaders all have their own version of what it is to lead and be a leader. *Creating Contagious Leadership* is intended to simplify the subject. As I was preparing to write this book, my wife Beverly kept reminding me about KISS (Keep It Short and Simple), so this book is what she calls an airplane read. It can be read on a medium-length trip.

Second, many leadership experts focus exclusively on the activities of a leader. We have list upon list of the things that successful leaders do to be successful. In *Creating Contagious Leadership*, I acknowledge the importance of doing the right things while advancing the notion that true leadership has more to do with who we are than what we do.

Finally, although many experts acknowledge that leadership has less to do with title and position today than in the past, there is also this pervasive attitude that some leaders are born and others have somehow developed their leadership skills in school. *Creating Contagious Leadership* offers the opinion that leadership, especially Contagious Leadership, is first and foremost a decision.

Creating Contagious Leadership is intended to be a road map for hiring, inspiring, developing and retaining leaders. I hope its simplicity will also stimulate thinking and debate. In its essence, leadership is not that difficult. The qualities and habits presented in this book can serve as a strong foundation for any leader in any organization, family, church or community. I have this image that creating Contagious Leadership is like boiling water. We start with a pot of cool water and then apply heat. In time, little bubbles begin to appear in the bottom of the pot. With consistent heat and more time, the tiny bubbles multiply exponentially. First there is one, then 2, 4, 16, 256. Before long the pot is full of raging hot molecules, all seemingly creating more hot molecules. This leadership "bubble effect" can be reproduced in any organization. Starting with employees, we begin to add heat (modeling the qualities and habits presented here). Over time, the employees begin to model the same qualities and habits. They become hot molecules by creating more Contagious Leaders. The process continues and spreads as long as the heat is applied. A culture of Contagious Leadership is created.

Over the past few years, a number of extraordinary companies have honored me by asking me to speak on the subject of *Creating Contagious Leadership* before their management teams and sales organizations. Companies like Wells Fargo Home Mortgage, GlaxoSmithKlein, ValPak, CIGNA, American Express and the University of Phoenix have given me the opportunity to work with leaders in their organizations who not only embrace the qualities and habits presented in *Creating Contagious Leadership* but, more importantly, model them daily. The Contagious Leaders in these organizations understand that creating a culture of contagious leadership inspires employees to be more fully engaged in the essential job of creating loyal customers who wouldn't think of taking their business elsewhere.

As simple as I have attempted to make this book, there are 9 habits and 13 qualities to learn, understand and model. Attempting to take these on all at once may be unwise. Allow me to suggest a more appropriate course of action. I suggest you read the book through one time. Then go back and pick one or two of the qualities and habits to begin modeling. Once you have those handled and the people in your organization begin to model them, you can pick one or two more and begin the process again.

It's really pretty simple, and you have nothing at all to lose. Heck, you might even begin to apply some heat under the cool water and create a few bubbles. These hot molecules just might begin to pass the heat on to others in your organization and leadership will begin to spread. You'll begin to notice that leadership can be contagious without being expensive or difficult to create. Before you know it, everyone will be stepping up and you'll have created Contagious Leadership.

Have fun!

Contents

Chapter 1

Contagious Leadership

*Effective leaders recognize that the ultimate test
of leadership is sustained success, which demands
the constant cultivation of future leaders.*

— Noel M. Tichy
Leader to Leader

The world is desperate for leadership. Everywhere we turn—in every business periodical we pick up, every news report we read, every radio and TV interview we are exposed to — some executive, community leader, educator or parent is advancing the call for more leadership. With each exposure, there seems to be a different point of view or an opposing definition of what leadership is and what constitutes a leader. No wonder there is so much confusion. We all think leadership is crucial to our businesses, our schools, our communities and our families, yet we have difficulty defining exactly what we seek. *Creating Contagious Leadership* is intended to overcome this challenge by putting leadership in perspective, placing some meat on its bones, defining it, and making it abundantly clear that creating an environment of Contagious Leadership is not only possible, it is absolutely necessary.

Allow me to begin with a simple idea: For leadership to be contagious, we must first abandon the notion that it is about what we *do*. Nothing could be farther from the truth. Leadership is, has always been, and always will be about who we *are*.

From the very first day I began working, I had a vision of working with companies that were rich with leaders. These leaders developed and nurtured more leaders by modeling and rewarding the qualities that set leaders apart. The process spread as leadership became contagious and everyone from the mailroom to the boardroom caught the leadership fever. It is from this vision that *Creating Contagious Leadership* was developed.

Contagious Leadership is both a way of thinking and a process. It involves deciding how the people in a business will conduct themselves. There are six steps to creating Contagious Leadership:

Step 1. Decide that leadership, not management, is the standard of effectiveness and performance throughout the organization.

Step 2. Make sure *every person* in the organization knows exactly what is expected from leaders. Contagious Leadership is not a term applied just to the "executives" or "higher-ups." Every single person throughout the organization can develop and model the qualities of Contagious Leaders.

Step 3. Inspire every person to model the behavior and attitudes that the organization expects of Contagious Leaders.

Step 4. Develop policies that support, rather than undermine, the qualities and habits of Contagious Leadership.

Step 5. Institute systems to recognize and reward the behavior, attitudes and qualities expected of Contagious Leaders.

Step 6. Define the primary role of leaders, at every level, as developing and nurturing future leaders.

High Return/No Cost

Contagious Leadership offers every organization huge returns at little or no cost. This can also be the bad news. You can't write a check to "Create Contagious Leadership" and produce these returns. It takes time, thought, thoughtfulness, consistency and transformational thinking. Breaking old habits and creating new, more effective behavior and attitudes is an enormous challenge in many organizations.

Business leaders generally interpret the term "investment" to mean financial investment. The absence of a significant financial investment will often reduce the perceived value of an initiative, resulting in lack of confidence and little or no commitment. We have been programmed to believe that the more we invest — the more dollars we put at risk — the more value a program has. We generally view investment as either high-risk/high-return or low-risk/low-return. Low-risk/high-return investments are generally looked upon with some degree of skepticism. It may make good sense that the more we put at risk, the more committed we become. We can easily become trapped into talking about more efficiently investing capital and treating the low-investment/high-return initiatives lightly. My wife Beverly and I were once exposed to a very attractive business model that offered a significant return of residual income with little or no front-end capital requirement. When we shared the concept with several highly successful entrepreneur friends, one critically proclaimed, "It can't be true! For any business to be worth doing, you have to risk losing at least $10 million!" Frequently, this way of thinking prevents us from seeing and acting on great opportunities. As Thomas Edison allegedly once said, "I seldom see a great opportunity until it ceases to be one."

It also seems that the simpler solutions are generally the ones overlooked. We have become a culture where "complex" tends to equate to "value." This is not always the case. As you'll see, creating Contagious Leadership is not expensive or complex. But it's not easy either. As Trina Paulus, author of *Hope for the Flowers*, said, "How does one become a butterfly? You must want to fly so much that you are willing to give up being a caterpillar."

How badly do you want leadership in your organization? How badly would you like leadership to be contagious? Make no mistake about it: Creating an environment of Contagious Leadership has enormous potential for any organization willing to make it happen. The returns are in the following areas:
- Reduced expense/attrition
- Enhanced communications
- More effective teamwork
- Positive employee morale
- Improved productivity
- Increased creativity
- The ability to attract and retain superior talent

Reduced Expense/Attrition

Over and over again, we hear it said that the most significant challenge facing 21st-century organizations is the ability to attract and retain talent. When you create Contagious Leadership, your employees at every level are happier, feel more appreciated, have a greater feeling of worth, and enjoy a heightened sense of contribution and belonging. The effect is reduced attrition, the cost of which, as we detail later in this chapter, can be significantly higher than most executives are willing to realize.

Enhanced Communications

What is the cost of poor communications? What is the impact of communications-related mistakes, low morale and the "rumor mill effect"? Since we generally express these costs in "soft dollars," we rarely give them the attention they deserve.

In an environment of Contagious Leadership, communication happens early, often and in congruence with the organization's goals, objectives and values. It reduces crisis situations and the low levels of productivity that occur when employees feel uncertain, unsure or insecure.

More Effective Teamwork

Building trust and unity across all functions, departments and regions is essential to effective teamwork. By developing the qualities of Contagious Leadership, every person will be more "count-on-able" and less likely to create or participate in turf wars. The resulting synergy and focus on the desired end result inspires every team member to perform at higher levels.

Improved Productivity

Contagious Leadership inspires optimism, clarifies expectations, reduces "water cooler chit chat," and encourages higher levels of performance through more consistent recognition for accomplishments rather than failures. It raises the "band of performance" by employee involvement in setting the high bar.

Increased Creativity

One of our corporate clients has experienced dramatic operating efficiencies just by asking for opinions and then listening and implementing ideas, many of which were so obvious as to lead to "why didn't we think of that" comments. The Contagious

Leadership environment this organization has begun to create has resulted in employees feeling as though it's safe to make suggestions, secure that the suggestions will be considered, implemented and valued because of the recognition they receive for their efforts.

Superior Talent

Corporate culture has become a very important issue. A Contagious Leadership environment will actually attract Contagious Leaders. Today's employees are just as interested in the quality of the work environment as they are the compensation package and job requirements. Employees at every level have become quite skilled at identifying the culture that suits them best. Contagious Leadership focuses on the individual, nurtures their strengths, rewards their leadership habits and qualities, and encourages them to develop other Contagious Leaders. This culture naturally attracts individuals who are dedicated to being Contagious Leaders. The return is enormous for any organization that is willing to embrace Contagious Leadership.

To create Contagious Leadership, each of us has to be a Contagious Leader. We can't sit back and wait for someone to make us contagious; it never works. Contagious Leadership is like the title of H. Jackson Brown, Jr.'s wonderful book, *Opportunity Dances with Those Already on the Dance Floor*. We have to model the behavior, attitudes and qualities common to Contagious Leaders. Each of us has to be contagious for it to spread.

How often have we heard CEOs and other top executives proclaim that people are the organization's greatest resource? It has become the CEO and HR battle cry worldwide. Unfortunately, all too many executives, managers and supervisors actually lead in a manner that is more consistent with Henry Ford's old philosophy: "When all I want is a good pair of hands, unfortunately I must take them with a person attached."

What's the plan to attract and keep the best people with this attitude as a core value? It's not creating Contagious Leaders, that's for sure! You have to nurture Contagious Leaders or they'll go somewhere where they *can* be nurtured. Hiring and keeping the best people is not always about which company pays the most.

I have concluded that there are two types of leaders: Contained and Contagious. Contained Leaders play small, always inside themselves, and usually focus more on protecting who they are and what they have rather than building an organization of leaders. At one time or another, we have all worked for or with a Contained Leader. They keep everything very close to the vest, guarding the information they value. They think this is the key to their power and authority. If they develop others, they do so to focus the spotlight on themselves — "See how great Tom is at developing his people? He'll go a long way around here." These efforts were all about Tom.

Contagious Leaders play full-out in everything they do and firmly believe that developing other Contagious Leaders is the only route to long-term success.

Jack Welch, former CEO of General Electric Company, may well have been the most Contagious Leader of all time. Perhaps you didn't like him personally or his methods, but you will have to admit that he successfully created other Contagious Leaders. He did so because it was the right thing to do for the company. He knew that, without this type of leadership throughout the company, GE would have been just another company struggling to carve out more market share, more revenue, and more return to shareholders. The best way for any company to stand out is to dare to actually be that which every other company only dreams of being — a Contagious Leadership factory.

Let's talk for a moment about how leaders are developed. First you become an employee. You could be an entry-level employee or an executive just starting with the company. In the beginning, we are all just employees!

Then you move on to being a manager. You're given your first opportunity to be responsible for the efforts of others. It's your first taste of what it's like to try to motivate someone other than yourself. If you do a good job and are lucky, someone becomes aware of the fact that your efforts to motivate the performance of others has worked at least as well as other people's, so they begin to think of you as a leader. Someone says, "That new fella down in marketing has real leadership qualities. I like the 'cut of his jib.'" It's sad but true that many companies "anoint" leaders in this very way. We also anoint leaders because of their ability to put out fires and manage a crisis.

Once you've been anointed a leader, you have two choices. You can be like most others and become a Contained Leader, and remain ever cautious. Or you can make a decision to step out, be your own person, and become a Contagious Leader.

Unfortunately, this decision isn't entirely up to you. The company also has something to say about it. If your organization has a culture where being "contained" is rewarded, it will be just a bit more of a challenge to step out and become contagious.

On the other hand, if the culture recognizes the qualities of a Contagious Leader, then stepping out puts you in very good company. There is also a third option: Your company prefers Contained Leadership but you have decided that it's not for you. You choose Door Number 3, the exit. You go in search of a company more suited to you, a place where you are more culturally compatible. Just be aware. In his wonderful book, *Topgrading*, Dr. Bradford D. Smart suggested that the full replacement cost of a $60,000 annual salary could be as much as $800,000. If this is even 50% accurate, Door Number 3 is a very expensive option. Good people are hard to find and very expensive to replace.

Contained Leadership vs. Contagious Leadership

I've made it my business to observe the behavior common to leaders, particularly Contagious Leaders. My understanding of these qualities is not based on any statistically significant sample taken in a controlled test. Rather, the qualities come from my 30+ years of working with and observing leaders. Decide for yourself if these qualities sound and feel right to you, and then decide to what extent you will commit to developing them in your organization. Remember that some of the characteristics are driven by company culture and some are driven by the individual.

Contagious Leaders have practiced and developed these nine habits that distinguish them from Contained Leaders:

1. Spotlighting — The habit of focusing attention, directly or indirectly, on the efforts and accomplishments of another person or group. For Contained Leaders, the spotlight is usually on themselves.

2. Cultivating Character — The habit of making responsible choices about "how" we do things not just "what" we do. For Contained Leaders, it is always about "what"— the numbers, the bottom line. It's rare when they consider the "how," because character rarely plays a role in decision-making. We'll cover the 13 character qualities that distinguish Contagious Leaders in Chapter 3.

3. Involved Recognition — The habit of articulating specific actions that deserve praise. Contained Leaders say "Good job, Harry." Contagious Leaders also tell Harry why and how he did a good job.

4. Looking to Greatness — The habit of emphasizing strengths. Contained Leaders focus on people's shortcomings and point them out as often as possible. Contagious Leaders recognize others' strengths.

5. Vibrant Communication — The habit of *effectively* exchanging information, thoughts and feelings that build unity and enhance productivity. "Keep 'em guessing" is what Contained Leaders are all about. "Tell 'em only what they need to know and not a moment before they need to know it." Contagious Leaders know there is nothing more important than communication. Open, honest communication will do more to improve morale and performance in most companies than almost any other strategy.

6. Unobstructed Vision — The habit of focusing actions on a clear and sensory-rich picture of the desired result. Contained Leaders only have a vague picture of where the company is going. Contagious Leaders can see the objectives clearly — and share the vision with others.

7. Touching Lives — The habit of truly knowing your most valuable asset — people. Contained Leaders avoid any real, deep involvement. Most don't know if the people reporting to them are married or single. They don't know the names of their employees' significant others, or the names and ages of their children, or even where they live. Contagious Leaders know all this and more, not because it's good for business, but because they truly care about their most important asset.

8. A Passionate Stand — The habit of being fully expressed. Contained Leaders are always controlled. Contagious Leaders step out onto "the skinny part of the branches."

9. Permission Mentoring — The habit of ripening aspiring Contagious Leaders. Contained Leaders want a staff of imitators and followers. They want people to do what they want them to do and to do it their way. Contagious Leaders want the concept of Contagious Leadership duplicated, but they allow individuals to do it their way. They duplicate their actions through others.

Cultural Compatibility —
The Benefits of Contagious Leadership

Attracting, developing and retaining good people is the principal challenge for most businesses in the new economy. This is true despite the fact that some sectors have recently experienced rather significant cutbacks. There are two primary causes for this: First, there are fewer of us entering the workforce, particularly in the 20-35 age range, which gives us a smaller talent pool from which to identify and nurture future leaders. Second, we have more choices than ever before. This is the 21st-century economy.

The key to this challenge is hiring the right people in the first place. Not just people with the right experience and education, but people who fit into the culture — one that nurtures, develops, supports and rewards the habits and qualities of Contagious Leadership. Two things are critical in this process. First, you must make the decision to nurture future Contagious Leaders and, second, you must decide to hire the right people, those who have made the decision to be Contagious Leaders, in the first place

My friend Joe Calloway, CSP, CPAE, author of *Becoming a Category of One: How Extraordinary Companies Transcend Commodity and Defy Comparison*, makes a profound point in his opening chapter. He talks about making the decision to be a leader, and he references the movie *Apollo 13*. At the end of the movie, Jim Lovell (played by Tom Hanks) is in his backyard with other astronauts, celebrating Neal Armstrong's walk on the moon. He kept staring at the moon and finally said to the others, "It wasn't a miracle. We just decided to go."

Deciding is a necessary first step to realizing the enormous performance benefits of developing a culture of Contagious Leadership. Just look at what Jack Welch did at GE. Leadership became the top priority when Welch took over, and the proof of its effectiveness is in the performance of the company. In 1981, GE had total assets of $20 billion and revenues of $27.24 billion. Its earnings were $1.65 billion. With 440,000 employees worldwide, GE had a market value of $12 billion. In 1997, revenues were $90.84 billion, with net earnings of $8.2 billion. According to their 1997 annual report, GE's market value was the highest in the world at $300 billion.

Equally impressive is the number of Contagious Leaders that GE nurtured during Welch's tenure who went on to lead other companies. More Fortune 500 CEOs came from the GE Contagious Leadership environment than from any other company in recorded history. GE, at least under Jack Welch's Contagious Leadership, was a leadership factory.

It is astounding what a company can accomplish with cultural compatibility, a clear vision of the future, and the decision and determination to create an environment of Contagious Leadership rather than a system bogged down in management.

Using the Nine Habits
for Creating Contagious Leadership

This book covers a great deal of territory. I suggest that you not allow yourself to get lost in all the detail in the first pass. Read the book all the way through. Begin thinking about what Contagious Leadership might look like in your department, your region or your entire organization. Keep in mind that creating Contagious Leadership is a process that starts with your culture. Changing a culture does not have to take forever, and it requires taking one step at a time. So I suggest that you carefully consider your jumping-off point. Then pick a place to begin. Frankly, any of the nine habits will do for most, because each of them needs to be fully developed, practiced and ingrained in your company culture. Every employee, from the boardroom to the mailroom, has to endorse the principles of Contagious Leadership. As you'll see in Chapter 12, "Contagious Leaders in Action," you don't have to be a corporate executive to be a Contagious Leader. Each of us, in our own ways, can practice these habits every day in everything we do — whether at work, at home, in the classroom, in our churches, or in our community activities. In Chapter 11, "Getting Started," we offer suggested strategies for developing and measuring each habit within your department or company. Regardless of where you choose to begin, the process will be the same. You'll need to develop, implement, practice, measure and reinforce each habit. The process can take eight months or eight years. It doesn't really matter. In the end, you will have created an environment where the days are not long enough, and every employee will begin each day excited because they no longer "have to" come to work, they "get to." Imagine how inspiring it will be when every employee wakes up each morning excited and eager to begin the day because they "get to" do yesterday all over again.

The Contagious Leadership fever spreads through you to others. Walter Lippmann perhaps said it best:

The final test of a leader is that he leaves behind him
in other men the conviction and the will to carry on.
— Walter Lippmann
New York Herald Tribune

Chapter 2

Habit #1: Spotlighting

*Spotlighting: The habit of focusing attention,
directly or indirectly, on the efforts and accomplishments
of another person or group.*

Spotlighting — what a wonderful word! It so aptly describes this powerful habit. If only I could take full credit for creating this leadership quality. The first time I heard the term was during a program called *Managing Goal Achievement*, put on by Integrity Systems, a training company in Phoenix, Arizona. Throughout the program, the facilitators demonstrated and continuously reinforced the value of spotlighting. Every time a participant would share something with the other participants, the facilitators would listen carefully. Then, when the participant was finished and had taken their seat, the facilitators would acknowledge the speaker for their comments. They didn't just say "nice job." They went beyond that and actually explained in detail what made the sharing so valuable for the others in the group and why the individual had made such a contribution. By the time the facilitator was finished, the participant felt as though a "spotlight" had really been on them, as if they had been honored for making a difference. They were made to feel that what they contributed had indeed been valuable, and they were placed on a pedestal as a shining example for all the others to model.

As I drove to and from the *Managing Goal Achievement* program each week, I considered how spotlighting so aptly described one of the habits of a Contagious Leader. Contagious Leaders have the unique ability of focusing attention on others, not just when they speak or contribute something, but all the time. The habit of spotlighting is really not unique, but the people who practice it are.

Spotlighting is an active process where one person focuses full attention on someone or on a group. In study after study of employee motivators, we learn that being heard — feeling as though what we say and do counts in an organization or to a manager or leader — is critically important. In my experience, it is not so much that employees are not heard or listened to, but that they don't *feel* like they are. The Contagious Leader uses spotlighting and has developed ways of shutting out all the distractions so others feel listened to. How many of us have worked for people who always allow distractions to interrupt our conversations? In the middle of a meeting, right when we are speaking about a key point, they take or make a phone call, or they go to their computer to check email. It is so disempowering! My wife Beverly once worked with a CEO who had a habit of doing this, but he attempted to justify it by bragging that he was unique and had this great ability to do many things at once. Baloney! What he had was the ability to make her feel as though what she had to contribute was worthless. After a while, because he insisted on proving this great ability over and over again, she stopped contributing. In this case, the spotlight was on him and not Beverly. It was all about his great ability rather than her contribution. This is just one example of a disease that has grown to epidemic proportions in many of today's corporations. Employees have simply stopped contributing. The greatest pool of creative ideas has dried up in many organizations because too many so-called leaders are determined to have the spotlight on them rather than on the person making the contribution.

The Benefits of Spotlighting

Direct spotlighting is an active process that can pay huge dividends and improve morale immediately at no cost. So *start listening!* Really actively listening. Give your full attention to every conversation. Make the person in front of you feel like they are the only person in the world, and carefully listening to what they have to say is the most important thing you could be doing. Look the person straight in the eye and don't stop until they have finished speaking. Stay present, don't allow yourself to be distracted: no paper shuffling, no phone calls, no side conversations, no interrupting, no asking questions and not waiting for the answer. It is most important that you clear your mind, stop thinking of other things, and actually get involved with the conversation. If someone (like your assistant or the CEO) attempts to interrupt your conversation, calmly explain that you are in an important conversation and can't be disturbed. When the person has finished speaking, acknowledge them for the contribution by recapping what they said in as much detail as possible. And, above all else, be sincere. Most employees can smell insincerity a mile away. It sounds simple enough, doesn't it? It isn't. This takes practice and commitment.

Here is what your organization will gain from spotlighting:

1. Every person with whom you communicate will immediately feel more appreciated, valued and worthwhile, regardless of the outcome of your communication.

2. Because they feel more valued, they will drop their guard and open up to more creative thinking and problem-solving.

3. As amazing as this may sound, you will immediately begin to know people better. They will tell you things about themselves that you wouldn't otherwise know. People who know each other have a better working relationship, make fewer mistakes, and spend less time bickering, less time clarifying instructions, and more time just getting the job done.

4. The habit of spotlighting will be modeled and duplicated throughout your organization. You won't have to ask anyone to do this either. They will just notice how empowered they feel and begin doing the same thing. That's contagious spotlighting!

Spotlighting can be equally effective in an indirect way, even though it is a more passive process. It involves giving detailed credit to another person or group even when they are not present. Notice I said "detailed credit." Indirect spotlighting is passive in the sense that the person or group is not present, but the process requires you to be very active in the accumulation of details for which this person or group is being acknowledged. This third-party acknowledgment can have a powerful effect on the performance of any department, region or company. The company grapevine may well be your most efficient form of communication. When the Contagious Leader tells a group in Denver what a terrific job the customer service department in Dallas is doing, the group in Dallas knows about it before the Contagious Leader has finished making the acknowledgment. The key is to be as specific, genuine and detailed as possible. Let me offer an example:

> *I know this is our quarterly sales meeting, but I wanted to take just a moment to tell you what's going on in the operations center in Dallas. Grace Schilling, the center manager, spent several days in one-on-one and small-group meetings with all the center employees to uncover more creative solutions for improving order processing and customer care. On the basis of these meetings, 23 new approaches were identified, and we've implemented all 23 initiatives. To date, processing time has improved 14%, and customer care has risen from 63% positive to 87% in just four weeks. Everyone working in the center deserves a great big thank you for their creativity, dedication and commitment to making us the #1 provider. Let's hear it for Grace Schilling and her team!*

Grace Schilling may not have known that the sales manager was going to say this. I promise you, however, that she and her team knew by the end of the day. How difficult was this? How long did it take? It took 45 seconds to say and perhaps less than an hour to research. How much impact do you think the acknowledgment had on Grace and her team, as well as other teams in the company?

There is one thing you might want to be a bit cautious about as you begin spotlighting, however. It is sad but true that most of us are not accustomed to being listened to or acknowledged, so when it occurs we can become a little nervous. As you carefully listen and focus your full attention on someone, they may be thinking: "Why is she looking at me straight in the eye, and why is she paying so much attention? She usually checks her email when we're talking. I wonder what's wrong? Is she mad at me?"

Just be cautious! It may take awhile for people to realize you have become a Contagious Leader. After all, many of us are accustomed to working with Contained Leaders who tend to take the spotlight and keep it all to themselves.

Contagious Leaders share the spotlight or they give it away completely. In fact, Contagious Leaders have a habit of sitting in the front row, applauding the accomplishments of others. Henry Miller was speaking about Contagious Leaders when, in *The Wisdom of the Heart*, he said, "The real leader has no need to lead — he is content to point the way."

Chapter 3

Habit #2:
Cultivating Character

Cultivating Character: The habit of making responsible choices about how *we* do things, not just what *we* do.

To be a Contagious Leader, character is essential. During many of my speaking programs about creating Contagious Leadership, I ask the question: How many of you think character is important?

In nearly every case, 100% of the audience raises their hand. No surprise here, right? Disagreeing with this premise is like disagreeing that baseball, apple pie, motherhood and the flag are symbols of America. I have asked executives, teachers, clergy, parents, and community leaders, and they all know that character is important.

Then I ask the really big question: What is character?

The answer is the same no matter where I go. It usually begins with a very long pause. Then the audience begins to look down at the floor. The pause turns into a blank stare and a perplexed look, sometimes even the look of sheer panic. This is a look that teachers throughout the world know all too well: the look of students who know they are supposed to know the correct answer but don't.

Most of us have some difficulty defining character. Frequently a well-placed executive will say, "I can't put words to it, but I sure know it when I see it." The trouble with this answer is that it is impossible to teach something we can't define, and it's impossible to model something we can't describe.

Ralph Waldo Emerson said, "Every great institution is the lengthened shadow of a single man. His character determines the character of the organization." He knew then what we know today. Character *does* count. The people at the top in most companies — who ultimately make all the hiring, firing and promotion decisions — believe that character is vital to the future success of their company. These executives may not be able to define character, but they instinctively know that employees with character make better employees, better managers, better communicators and better future executives. Moreover, they suspect that employees with character remain with the company longer, thereby reducing turnover, which can be an enormous drain on earnings.

My research into leadership and character has not involved any focus groups or double-blind studies with control groups. Rather, for years, I have studied Contagious Leaders — those who make us feel good being around them, who make us feel as though we can accomplish anything, who make us believe we have something worthwhile to contribute. I also identified a handful of people who had an impact on my life and reviewed what they had in common.

Through my personal observation and research, I developed a system for defining, measuring and integrating character into any culture and performance-review system. If every executive, manager, supervisor and employee would use their valuable time and resources to understand and use this system, leadership would indeed become contagious.

Character is not one thing, but rather the sum of 13 distinct qualities. Defining character is rather like defining a wonderful meal. Is it the wine that defines the meal? Or the entrée, or the dessert, or the service? You can't define the meal without considering the whole. Together, the 13 elements defined below make up character. I have not presented them in any particular order of importance because most people will rank them differently anyway.

• Attitude

Attitude drives everything else. Not just a positive attitude, but a "can-do" attitude: *I can do that! I can learn math, science, English, geometry, the new software program! I can play that game! I can show up on time for meetings! I can complete that proposal! I can do a better job!*

Contagious Leaders have contagious attitudes. Keith Harrell, CSP, CPAE, writes about it in his book, *Attitude is Everything.* It *is* everything and it's one of the qualities of a Contagious Leader that is simple to model. Notice I didn't say "easy." Attitude is a matter of choice: We can either have a contagious attitude or a contained attitude. Either way, the people we work with will model us. The question is: Which attitude do we want modeled and which alternative is most effective in obtaining the results we're looking for?

Scott Ostrander is a great example of the power of a contagious attitude. In 2001, he became general manager of a relatively new resort and club in Arizona. The club opened in late 1999 and had been struggling to increase membership and use. It is a spectacularly beautiful facility, with breathtaking views, world-class tennis facilities, well-run full-service spa, and a first-class restaurant. Despite its amenities and features, however, the club was struggling.

When it opened just prior to Thanksgiving 1999, all the management and staff were full of anticipation, excitement and possibility. Just a year later, there was uncertainty in their eyes and lack of enthusiasm in the way they carried themselves, greeted people, and cared for members and guests. Enter Scott Ostrander.

Scott Ostrander's contagious attitude lets him see everything as possible and always makes people feel as though his job is not a job at all, but a reward. He always smiles, always walks at 100 miles an hour, always has his plate completely full, and always has time to chat. He uses spotlighting and firmly believes that recognition is the great motivator. He quickly began recognizing staff for all the little things that had previously gone unnoticed. During his inspiring and fun-packed monthly employee meetings, he changed the way the employee-of-the-month was rewarded. Scott recognized that some employees had direct and frequent contact with members and guests, while others had no contact but were equally critical to achieving the club's mission. He instituted two employees-of-the-month, a Front-of-the-House employee (with contact) and a Heart-of-the-House employee (with little or no contact). Within months of his arrival, the spirit of the staff had been completely altered. Members were once again excited, and the club was on its way toward new renovations, an expansion program and great success.

To be sure, Scott Ostrander brought other skills and experience to his position. In fact, he was so strong that he was recruited away by another property. It is interesting to note that the thing the members and staff miss the most is his attitude.

• Authenticity

My friend and colleague, Dr. Carl Hammerschlag, once told a group of professional speakers: "Authenticity occurs when the head and the heart meet at the lips; when what we think and what we feel is congruent with what we say and do."

Oh, how the world is desperate for authenticity! Might we have viewed the challenges that many organizations have had in recent years just a bit differently if the leaders had been more authentic from the start?

Being authentic is about knowing and being true to who we are, not who we pretend to be or who others would have us be. Many individuals have been acting the part of the successful executive or manager for so long that they have forgotten who they really are. Did you know that 40% of corporate executives would change careers if they could maintain their current income level? Many have just gotten tired of not being true to themselves, of being in jobs and cultures that require them to be other than who they are. I see it all the time in the workshops and seminars I conduct on *Leadership Communications and Leadership Selling*. We use behavioral profiles to help managers and leaders understand their natural and adapted behavioral styles. Many have been so overly adapting to their supervisor, the job, or the company culture for so long that they don't even realize the level of stress it puts on their performance. During the course of the program, it becomes abundantly clear that, although some adapting may be appropriate, to be a consistent winner over the long haul, being authentic is the place to start.

I'll never forget the first time my brother Bart and I displayed the running shoes he had developed for the Hersey Custom Shoe Company. We had set up a booth at Hynes Auditorium in Boston on the weekend prior to the Boston Marathon. All the runners had to register at the Hynes and had to walk through the auditorium, where manufacturers and suppliers of athletic/running equipment and apparel had displayed their products. The Hersey Custom Shoe Company had been in business for only a few weeks, and we were so excited. As I reflect on the weekend, it brings a big smile to my face. Here we were: me, the advertising agency executive, and Bart, the shoemaker, standing behind this booth talking to the finest runners in the world, not one of whom was over 6 feet tall or weighed more than 150 pounds. Bart and I weighed 150 pounds in the fifth grade. He is 6'5"+ and, at the time, weighed well over 270 pounds. He had a full beard, and he wore jeans and a plaid lumberman's shirt. He rather resembled a tall, heavy version of Robert Redford in the movie *Jeremiah Johnson*. A friend once said he looked like Montana — not the former football player, but the state. As we walked around the show, we saw all these slight, fit, beautiful people manning most of the other booths. At the time, neither Bart nor I was slight, fit or beautiful. Neither were we runners. Bart was, and still is, one of the most talented shoemakers you'll ever meet. It never occurred to him to be anything but who he was: a shoemaker who had developed, and could make, custom shoes that helped distance runners go longer, farther, more comfortably and with less chance of injury. He wasn't a runner, just a great shoemaker. He was, and has always been, authentic. His success soared. The runners loved his contagious authenticity as much as they loved his great shoes. And they still do — he is definitely contagious.

• Contribution

Contagious Leaders are about making things better. They make a difference in their companies, communities, families, and churches, and in the lives of the people they work with. Once in a while, we all need a helping hand or a little pick-me-up from a colleague when we get tired and frustrated.

Consider Lim Hayes at the Carrolton Elementary School in Carrolton, Texas. The school gave this little man from Cambodia a going-away party. The mayors from the neighboring towns of Carrolton and Farmers Branch gave speeches, and over 1000 kids enthusiastically applauded Lim Hayes.

So, you may ask, what's the big deal? Well, when was the last time you heard of a school or a company throwing a going-away party for the head custodian?

These people loved Lim Hayes because, since coming to this country many years ago, his life had been about making a difference for the kids — making a contribution. It may sound silly or old-fashioned, but today, more than ever, employees and customers are responding to Contagious Leaders whom they know will be there to make a difference. Contribution isn't something Contagious Leaders do opportunistically. They are about making a difference all the time.

• Commitment

Contagious Leaders make deep commitments. They are not committed just when it *suits* them. They believe that people are either in or they are out. When they are in, they are in for the duration. Even when their business is not going as well as they would like, they ask, "What can I do to make it better" not "Where can I go to find a better deal?"

Steve Chandler, author of *100 Ways to Motivate Yourself* and *Reinventing Yourself*, makes a wonderful distinction between owners and victims. He says owners — those of us who take full responsibility for our lives and our businesses — treat commitment like a decision. Victims treat commitment like it's a feeling that will pass. Victims have a tendency to place blame, and more often than not, they have someone else to point the finger at, to make wrong. Owners, on the other hand, say, "I realize we have challenges, but I've made a decision. So what can I do to improve the situation?"

• Determination

In 1941, Winston Churchill was asked to deliver the graduation address at his high school alma mater. The auditorium was crowded but silent as parents, teachers and students waited to hear this historic treasure pass on his insights to the graduates. He stood, slowly walked across the platform, faced the silent crowd, and said, "Never, never, never, never, never give up." Determination is a quality of Contagious Leadership. While not blind to potential setback, Contagious Leaders become even more determined in the face of adversity. They dig in, consider alternatives, become more creative, and think and act "outside the box." In our world, where commitment has become a "when it serves my purpose" philosophy, it's easy to give up, avoid difficult tasks and situations, and move on when the going gets tough. By modeling determination, Contagious Leaders have a profound effect on their organizations and the lives of the people around them.

• Discipline

Aristotle said, "What it lies in our power to do, it lies in our power not to do." Each of us has this awesome power. The space between "to do and not to do," that small gap, is where discipline resides. Sometimes the discipline to use that power, to develop and execute plans, is the difference between succeeding and failing. I just finished reading *Execution, The Discipline of Getting Things Done* by Larry Bossidy and Ram Charan. Oh, how many organizations and individuals have come up short for lack of execution. Between the lines in this wonderful book, readers were reminded again and again that it takes discipline to execute. Consistently succeeding at *any* game takes great discipline. It is the mortar between the bricks and serves as insurance against becoming lethargic and uninspired. Discipline is the "stuff" of which greatness is made. Discipline separates Contagious Leaders from all others.

We must be careful to remember that, as with all the other Contagious Leadership qualities, it is possible to use discipline for all the wrong reasons. The illegal and unethical activities for which many organizations have been called on the carpet in recent years also took great discipline to create and execute. Contagious Leaders understand this important distinction.

• Drive

The drive of Contagious Leaders is quite different from determination or discipline. It lies deep inside each of us. It is the reason we get up every morning and keep going back to our jobs, whatever they are. Although some of us are highly motivated by money, drive usually goes beyond the money. If drive is just about the money, then we live in a "have to," not a "get to" world. Sure we all want to make more money. But that's not what drive is all about. I tell you from experience: "have to" is a lot harder and less fun than "get to."

In the *Leadership Communication and Leadership Selling* workshops I mentioned earlier, we also use a values profile. It measures the six attitudes, interests and values that we all have in differing blends. It is fascinating to discuss these with participants, particularly those people who think of themselves as money-driven but who aren't really. Many are driven by learning or contribution or principles and values. Once we understand which of these values most strongly drives our behavior, it is amazing how free we become to be authentic.

Some time ago, I learned a value lesson about drive from my 18-year-old nephew, Shane. We were discussing his passion for mountain biking and how he picks up speed, going faster and faster, to jump over rocks, boulders, tree stumps or any number of other objects. I asked Shane why he risked life and limb to do this.

He told me it was the "adrenaline rush."

He said that when he tries a new jump, he's usually quite scared, sometimes even terrified. So he rides around and around in circles on his bike, building up speed. He does this over and over again, riding around and around, building speed and getting right to the object he will jump over, and then he stops. Build speed and then stop, build speed and then stop. Finally, he builds sufficient speed and confidence to take it all the way and jump over the object.

He said that with each jump comes a moment, usually when he's airborne, when he experiences the adrenaline rush — that one moment when he is both terrified and exhilarated at exactly the same time. And as he prepares for each jump, as he rides around and around picking up speed, he tries to remember the rush.

Shane knows his drive, his adrenaline rush. He knows how it feels and what it takes for him to create it. He knows his drive so well that he looks for opportunities to create it in other aspects of his life as well. He said, "And you know what, I even do it when I ask girls out for a date. I try to imagine the moment when I'm exhilarated, usually when I pop the question — and when I'm terrified, usually while I'm waiting for the answer." This 18-year- old not only knows his drive, but he has learned how to tap into it whenever he likes.

The big question is: What is your drive? What is your adrenaline rush? What gets you up in the morning and keeps you coming back? Contagious Leaders know their drive and the drive of those they work with. Do you "have to" get up every morning or do you "get to"?

• Embracing Change

Contagious Leaders embrace and participate in change. Some even revel in it and look for it. And, more often than not, they cause the change that usually disturbs Contained Leaders. It has been said that we can only count on two things in our lives —

death and taxes. Recent experience suggests that we can comfortably add change to the list. We can count on it like the sun rising in Arizona. Fighting change wastes valuable energy. Using that energy to make our jobs, departments and companies more productive and successful is the way of Contagious Leaders.

The way we handle change determines how others handle it, we can be certain of that. Every time you find yourself fighting change, any change, ask yourself if you would like to do your job with the equipment, materials and technology from 30 years ago. Do you think teachers would actually prefer teaching with 30-year-old textbooks? Would an administrative assistant actually prefer going back to an IBM Selectric typewriter and no email? How would you like to revert back to no cell phones, no Internet, no ATMs? Of course you wouldn't! We all want the benefits of change, we just don't want to go through the process.

I recently heard a speaker say that 96% of change is forced and 4% is initiated. I'm not sure these percentages are accurate, but let's assume for a moment that they are. Is it any wonder we have such a strained relationship with change? Rather than fighting change, Contagious Leaders just alter the equation. They initiate change or, at the very least, embrace it.

• Focus

My wife Beverly says, "In most companies, idea people are valued, but implementers are priceless." We all experience so many distractions that it's difficult to stay focused, stay on plan, stay on track. How many organizations have failed for lack of focus? Despite brilliantly developed and articulated strategic plans, many organizations just don't get the job done. We can call it failure to execute or lack of follow-through but, at the end of the day, focus was lost, distractions prevailed, and goals were not achieved. Contagious Leaders — implementers — have the ability to remain focused no matter what.

A friend told me a story that speaks to the downside of not

being focused. We were discussing this book, and he told me that his company had grown at a rate of 25% each year for five consecutive years. The founder and chairman operated from a philosophy that if everyone just did their job and tended to the customer, everything else would take care of itself. Then, after all this growth and success, one of the people who had been with the company from the beginning, someone who had helped create this company, gained some control and began to shift the focus. He had a financial background and believed that the company needed to be more intelligent about its resources. After all, they couldn't expect to grow at a rate of 25% every year, could they?

As this new philosophy of watch-every-nickel-and-keep-a-tight-control-on-your-expenses took hold and began to spread, the company's growth began to slow and finally turned south. It took several years to reverse the trend. As my friend said, "We stopped focusing on what was really important. We started to just hold on. We were playing to keep from losing rather than playing to win."

I used to see this philosophy at work when I was in the advertising business. It was as if the brand manager or advertising director or CEO would get bored with one direction and move on to another, not giving the first plan an opportunity to succeed. "Branding" seems to be today's buzz word. Every wannabe marketing expert is writing and speaking on branding. What's the big deal? Is branding actually a new subject? Of course it isn't! Branding is just determining who or what the brand is and then expressing that with rigorous attention to detail and consistency day in and day out. When I worked with the great people at The Stanley Works — people like Don Davis, the former chairman; Fran Hummell, advertising director; and Bill Axline, vice president of sales and marketing in the tool division and later general manager for the door division — we would occasionally add a person to the creative team to keep our creative edge. It rarely failed that this new person would want to make some change, in part to make the advertising better but sometimes just to make their mark. More often than not, they wanted to make the logo smaller. (I never did meet a client who liked having their logo made smaller.) It was the great advertising we created and the consistent focus on the details that helped make Stanley the brand of choice for millions worldwide. It is knowing who we are and then sticking to our strategy that separates great from good and contagious from contained. Contagious Leaders have a well-developed ability to stay focused.

• Integrity

Integrity isn't just about telling the truth. Integrity is about being our word, every day and in everything we do. Not just when it serves us, but particularly when it doesn't. Integrity is about being on time.

A November 26, 2002, article in *USA Today* entitled "Late, I'm Late: Survey finds CEOs tardy 60% of the time" made the point quite clearly: "Tardiness is a chronic problem among chief executive officers. They arrive late for 6 in 10 meetings, according to a survey of 2,700 CEOs released in September (2002) by management consulting firm Proudfoot." Being late is not only a time-waster, it also shows a lack of integrity and demoralizes the troops. How much time is wasted in your company by rounding up all the players for meetings? Think about what this must cost in soft dollars. According to this *USA Today* article, "If Citigroup CEO Sanford Weill arrives 15 minutes late to a meeting with his 4 best-paid lieutenants, it costs the company $4,250." Even if you are not in charge of Citigroup, what is the cost of your lack of integrity — arriving late for meetings? Let's say your company or department has 3 meetings a day and, on average, there are 5 attendees. If just one arrives 10 minutes late, that is 4 people wasting 2 hours every day, 10 hours every week, 43 hours each month at 4.3 weeks in a month, 516 hours every year. Let's assume that the average annual salary, without benefits and overhead allocation, of these 5 attendees is $50,000. This 10-minute lack of integrity is costing your company $48 per day, $240 per week, $1,041 per month and $12,384 per year, all because one person was 10 minutes late for 3 meetings a day. If your company employs 50 people this is the equivalent of hiring 1 extra person just to sit around and do nothing.

Please don't misunderstand: Integrity is not just about being on time, and Contagious Leaders don't practice integrity just because it saves the company money. It is not always about dollars and cents. More often than not, it's just the right thing to do.

• Motivation

I am often asked if I am a motivational speaker. Here is the truth about motivation: No one can motivate another person. I may think I'm a pretty darn good speaker, but down deep I also know that I can't motivate someone else. A CEO can't motivate employees. Parents can't even motivate their own children. Motivation has to come from within. As Contagious Leaders, our job is to be role models for motivation.

There are three types of motivation: fear, incentive and causal. Fear and incentive motivation never work, at least not for very long, because the stimuli (either fear or incentive) need to be constantly present. Take away the fear (you'll be fired if you don't measure up) or the incentive (you could win this month's sales contest and the trip to Tahiti) and nothing happens, because there is no motivation.

Causal motivation is about working to be the best we can be without any outside stimuli. Contagious Leaders don't wait for external motivation. They make things happen, and by doing so, they model behavior that creates an environment that encourages self-motivation.

Barbara Jean Patterson, a 75-year-old Minneapolis actress, drama coach and retired teacher, knows about motivation. She dragged a boy out of the hall one day because she needed some talent for the high school's production of *West Side Story*. The boy she grabbed didn't want to participate, lacked motivation and was headed down the wrong path. Barbara Jean Patterson saw something in the boy that he could not see in himself. The production, and Barbara Jean's inspiration, helped the boy realize that life was up to him. The parents of this boy credit Barbara Jean with saving his life, and he has publicly thanked her on many occasions. The boy, now a man, is international film star Gary Sinise.

Barbara Jean Patterson says: "We teach science so we know how to live life; we teach the arts so we know how to live life well." To Barbara Jean Patterson, living life well is a choice driven by self-motivation. Contagious Leaders like Patterson live by that old adage, "If it's to be, it's up to me."

• Creating Possibility

For any circumstance, challenge or effort, there are three possible sandboxes in which we get to play every day: the "what-has-been box," the "what-is box," and the "what-could-be box."

In the "what-has-been box" is everything we have ever learned. We visit this box to resolve familiar challenges. People who choose to play in the "what-has-been box" will say, "I can't do anything about that; it's the way we've always done it."

The "what-is box" is where we go to settle. People who choose to play in the "what-is box" will say, "I can't do anything about that; it's just the way things are."

The "what-could-be box" is where Contagious Leaders play. This is where possibility lives. In this box is a blank canvas. Every day we get to pull out the contents of this box and create our own masterpiece.

Certain behaviors will be used to play in each of these sandboxes. Which set of behaviors do you want modeled in your organization? Which behaviors do you choose to model?

• Risk

Wayne Gretsky, the greatest hockey player of all time, once said, "You miss 100% of the shots you never take." The willingness to take risks — not to be reckless, but to risk — separates Contagious Leaders from all others. Anything worth doing involves risk. Consider this for a moment:

RISK
To laugh is to risk appearing the fool,
To weep is to risk appearing sentimental,
To reach out for another is to risk involvement,
To expose feelings is to risk exposing your true self,
To place your dreams before a crowd is to risk their loss,
To love is to risk not being loved in return,
To live is to risk dying,
To hope is to risk despair,
To try is to risk failure.
But risk must be taken,
because the greatest hazard in life is to risk nothing.
The person who risks nothing
does nothing, has nothing, and is nothing.
They may avoid suffering and sorrow,
but they cannot learn, feel, change, grow, love, or live.
Chained by their certitudes,
they are slaves; they have forfeited their freedom.
Only a person who risks is free.
— Anonymous

Taking on the Character of a Contagious Leader

I mentioned in the first chapter that there is a lot of information in this book and suggested that you consider taking it slow. The 13 qualities we've discussed make up a nice, neat little package. Take on one per month, practice them, model them, and reward those that demonstrate Contagious Leadership. In just over a year, you will have positively altered your culture if you are doing this companywide and your own behavior if you are working on your own behalf.

On page 116, there is a self-assessment that will help you measure where you are now with regard to each quality, and will also help you track your progress and the progress of every person in your department, region or company.

Make sure you set goals for incorporating these qualities into your job descriptions and performance-review systems too. Through the self-assessment system, you can decide at what level you want each quality to be. For example, you may decide that, for your company, the standard for risk needs to be an 8 on the 10-point scale. You may also decide that vice presidents and above need to be at least a 7 to qualify for the bonus pool, while non-salaried employees can fall in an acceptable range between 5 and 7. It is your company, your department. You can create your culture to be whatever you decide. The important thing is to decide and to let people know what the new standards are. Finally, measure and reward, measure and reward. Creating Contagious Leadership is an evolution. It doesn't happen because you or the CEO mandates it. Contagious Leadership happens when individuals cultivate character, model the habits and qualities of Contagious Leaders every day, and frequently recognize these behaviors in others. The Contained Leader who believes they can write a memo or email declaring that the company now stands for Contagious Leadership and expect everyone to wear their assigned Contagious Leadership t-shirts to work every Friday and their Contagious Leadership lapel pins the rest of the time is in for a very big surprise.

Take it on! What have you got to lose? So your company converts only 50% of the Contained Leaders to the Contagious Leadership team. What a shame!

Chapter 4

Habit #3: Involved Recognition

Involved Recognition: *The habit of articulating specific actions that deserve praise.*

It is so simple. Why don't we all see it? Recognition has always been the simplest and easiest way to appreciate and value employees and customers, instill a sense of commitment to the company or brand, and inspire higher levels of performance. It is true for all of us. When a customer or manager tells us how terrific we are, what a great job we did, how we contributed to a particular group or audience, and what a difference we made, we feel better, communicate better and perform better, don't we? So why are there three forms of recognition instead of just the one that works best?

1. Contained Recognition. It should come as no surprise that Contained Leaders use contained recognition. This backhanded form of recognition is actually intended to turn the spotlight back onto the Contained Leader. We might hear the Contained Leader, particularly when he or she is speaking in front of their own superiors, say something like:

> *My staff have all done a terrific job this quarter. As a result, sales for the region have once again surpassed forecast. This is the fourth quarter in a row that our sales have exceeded the forecast. I have asked my staff to keep up the great work and work hard to go for five quarters in a row!*

Embedded in this offhand attempt at recognition is a sales pitch to the higher-ups. In a not-so-subtle way, this manager has announced what a terrific job she or he has done. The attempt to inspire another quarter of big results is simply a ploy to call more attention to the fact that she or he has delivered big results for four consecutive quarters. Can't you just hear the unsaid, "Now, isn't that worth a big raise and a promotion to VP huh boss, isn't it, huh, huh?"

2. Charismatic Recognition. I have heard this referred to as "lots of puff and no pastry." Charismatic leaders are not really leaders at all. They employ old-fashioned motivational pump-em-up strategies because they just don't have it in them to genuinely lead. Being a Contagious Leader takes work, determination and discipline — all those qualities we discussed in Chapter 3. It takes the ability to make tough decisions, inspire through action rather than words, and gain the endorsement of other leaders through commitment and dedication rather than speeches, memos and emails. For sure, Contagious Leaders have a measure of charisma. In fact, some of the great Contagious Leaders have lots of charisma. But that is just one component of the person. The charismatic leader has nothing but charisma.

The charismatic leader might call all the "troops" together and deliver the following message:

> *When I came to this region one year ago, I saw a group of talented people chomping at the bit to strut their stuff, to prove to the rest of the company that they could stand alone on top of the mountain, to be the leading region in the company. I believed in you, you believed in you, and for four consecutive quarters, you have stood alone — the best. Now we need to set our sights on higher ground. There are other mountains to climb, other forecasts to surpass, other goals to achieve. Each of you is an inspiration to me. Your dedication and determination, your clarity of purpose, your resolve to reach the top inspires us all to stand alone atop a new mountain. Blah, blah, blah. Blah, blah, blah. Blah, blah, blah.*

3. Involved Recognition. Contagious Leaders actively practice the habit of involved recognition. They know that to say, "Great job, Harry!" is simply not enough. "Great job, Harry" said over and over again becomes like city noise. When I first moved to the North End of Boston from the suburbs, the city noise kept me awake all night. There was traffic all the time, cars everywhere. People stayed up until all hours of the night, and I could hear them beneath my window. The noise of taxis and police and fire sirens added to my sleeplessness. After a few weeks, I no longer heard the sounds. It was as if the noise had abated. It hadn't, but it seemed that way. The way we speak to one another is just like city noise. After a while, we just don't hear it. We just don't pay much attention to the boss' half-hearted attempts at recognition. The Contagious Leader knows that, to be heard, to be effective, to continuously inspire higher levels of performance, the recognition must go deeper. We all (some more than others) have an insatiable appetite for praise. It becomes like a drug; we need more and more to achieve the same effect. Contagious Leaders fill that need. They not only recognize what you accomplished, but how it was accomplished, why it was accomplished, and the impact of the accomplishment.

A Contagious Leader might say:

I've never seen anything like this — four consecutive quarters of smashing the sales forecast and being the top sales team in the company. To each of the sales managers — Bill, Bob and Beverly — thanks so much for the training and dedication to teaching the entire field the value of raising our standards for our customer service. Look at the dividends — happier, more valued customers who purchase more and more of our brands.

To each of you in the field — Bob in New England, Joe in the Mid-Atlantic, Harry in New York, Mike in the Mid-West, Mark in Phoenix and the Southwest, and Bill on the West Coast — thanks for being open to new strategies for serving our customers, and for helping us all realize that doing a better job in the wrong areas doesn't work anymore. Thanks for making our customers feel so valued.

To Joan, Jim, Gail and Joel in sales support and

administration, thanks for making it possible for the field to raise the standards. And finally, to Bob, Milly, Megan, Kate, Jack and Jill in our warehouse, thanks for taking on the mission of improving our delivery and service, making us the very best in the category.

As a team, you have all taken on an impressive challenge and delivered amazing results. You should be proud of yourselves and your accomplishments. But now comes the hard part, believe it or not. Getting to the top is only half our battle; staying there is the other. We got this far by deciding to be the best and then delivering on that decision every day. Together we can decide to take this to any level we choose. Thanks for making such a difference.

How tough was that? How much more time did that statement take? And do you see how genuine it was? It wasn't about the leader, it was all about them — the people who did the work and deserve the recognition. The Contagious Leader publicly cited each person for their efforts and contribution. The spotlight was on each person in a detailed way that says to them and everyone around them that the Contagious Leader knows what they did and cares enough to point it out to the rest of the team. Do you think this type of behavior will be modeled throughout the region? You bet it will. Do you think this type of behavior will have a positive impact on performance? You bet it will.

Let me give you a real example of a Contagious Leader using involved recognition in an introduction. The Contagious Leader is Naomi Rhode CSP, CPAE, and she was asked to introduce Dianna Booher, MA, CSP, CPAE, at one of the concurrent sessions at the 2001 National Speakers Association convention.

This is just going to be an awesome session. I'm so thrilled to be able to introduce Dianna Booher. She is just absolutely awesome. I'd like you to grab on to your seat and say, "I will not budge. If I do, someone is going to grab it." It is a privilege to introduce Dianna the author, Dianna the speaker, Dianna the business woman, and by far the most important, Dianna the person.

Perhaps you will be impressed as I start to list some of the things she has done. Would it impress you if you knew she has written 39 books and the 40th is under contract? And, would you be a tad impressed if those books were in 10 languages? With major publishers? And she has 11 videos and 3 audios, 2 of which are with Nightingale-Conant, and 12 of which include software CDs. She has 12 more books under contract, and 11 book club selections in some of the major book clubs in America. And she is a syndicated columnist with 7 major publishing awards. Some of her main book titles are E-Writing — 21st Century Tools for Effective Communication; Communicate with Confidence — How to Say it Right the First Time and Every Time; and Get a Life without Sacrificing Your Career, which sounds like a very good idea to me.

She is an incredible author, and that is our focus. However, I think it is very important for you to know that NSA has abused Dianna Booher in a sense. We have abused her in that we have asked her to speak almost exclusively on authorship when she is a profound presenter. Dianna has spoken throughout this country. Her company is engaged by 227 of the Fortune 500 companies for speaking and for training. This is enough to make you gasp. Some of the titles of her speeches are From the Information Age to the Communication Age, Gender Communication, Did You Hear What I Think I Said?; and 10 Cs. Dianna the speaker is phenomenal.

Dianna the businesswoman is president of Booher Consultants, a communications training firm offering courses in writing, oral presentations, interpersonal skills and personal productivity, and she is an incredible businesswoman.

But it is Dianna the person that I really want to treat you with, because I believe that the person is the message. Dianna the person is wife, mother and grandmother, but you won't believe it when you see her. She is a woman of integrity; she is a woman of faith; she is a woman of genius. She's a woman of impact who changes the world by her thoughts, by her writing, by her speaking, by her business, and by the way she walks. With great privilege, I introduce to you my friend and my Speakers Roundtable colleague, Dianna Booher.

Granted, this is an introduction of a friend at a convention. But a Contained Leader would have read Dianna's standard introduction as requested. Not Naomi Rhode. She took it deeper, a lot deeper. She introduced Dianna the author, the speaker, the businesswoman, the friend. How long did it take to prepare this introduction? Who knows and who cares? It made a difference to Dianna Booher, and as one of the attendees at that session, it made an enormous impact on the way I listened to Dianna. Here it is two years later, and I still maintain that this is a great example of involved recognition.

The Benefits of Involved Recognition

The benefits of involved recognition are so obvious and simple that they are scary. Want to increase morale? Spotlight people as often as possible and use involved recognition. Want to increase productivity without cost? Spotlight people as often as possible and use involved recognition. Want to raise the self-esteem of each member of your team so they are genuinely excited about how they "get to" be on your team and participate in your programs and initiatives? Spotlight people as often as possible, use involved recognition, and coach others to practice the habits of spotlighting and involved recognition. This is Employee Motivation 101, but most managers, as well as contained and charismatic leaders, are in such a rush to get to the advanced material that they fail to practice the material that really works day in and day out.

Putting It into Practice

Just as with spotlighting, your employees, especially those who know you best, will probably be a bit taken back by the abrupt shift in your posture, so to speak. Give them time. This may be a new you and they'll need some time to adjust. Here are a few suggestions for easing your transition to practicing the habit of involved recognition:

1. Pay attention. Start looking for opportunities to practice involved recognition. You'll find they are all around you if you just open your eyes, ears and heart. Devote the next week to listening and observing behaviors, actions, efforts or accomplishments that deserve recognition. Look for opportunities by focusing on what people are doing well; look to their greatness. Not only will you find some wonderful accomplishments to recognize, but you'll have a far more enjoyable week as well.

2. Do it NOW. Involved recognition produces the most dramatic impact when used as close to the event that is being recognized as possible. One of our clients plans their annual sales conference as close to the end of the year as possible. Every salesperson is waiting to learn who delivered the big numbers. If the annual sales meeting is scheduled for April, the news is old by the time it is delivered. Remember the efficiency of the grapevine? In the case of our client, they literally learn who delivered the big numbers on Thursday afternoon and present the results the very next day.

3. Go public. The more public, the more impact. It's that simple. But be careful here. Not everyone likes being singled out for recognition or the spotlight. If you have an employee who genuinely dislikes attention, choose a different strategy, like sending a handwritten note to their home thanking them for their tremendous effort and accomplishments.

4. Spotlight. Make sure the spotlight is about the person or group being recognized. You would be better off not doing anything at all than risking the possibility of giving recognition to the wrong person or group.

5. Get specific. The more specific, the better. Harry wants to know what he did to deserve this recognition, as well as the impact it had on the customer, department, region and company.

Suggested Strategies

We have all heard that it takes 21 days to break or create a new habit — 21 days of practicing the habit, over and over again, constantly reminding ourselves of our commitment to the new habit. Before something new comes naturally to us, we have to force it a bit. When we first learned to tie our shoes, we would sit on the end of our bed and think, "OK, what's next? Shoes, that's it, I need to tie my shoes. So, the left goes over the right and then under, pull tight, make a loop with the right . . . ." Through practice, we no longer have to think about it. The same is true with the habit of involved recognition.

You may wish to identify several specific strategies for practicing involved recognition. I am offering a few suggestions below just to stimulate your thinking. Allow yourself and your team members to be as creative as possible. The opportunities are everywhere.

1. Employee meetings. Decide right now that from this moment forward, you will begin every employee meeting with involved recognition. You'll be amazed with the results. First of all, you'll begin to see and hear more things that are worthy of recognition by looking to greatness. Second, there will be more creativity, and more out-of-the-box thinking and acting at these meetings than you ever thought possible.

2. Employee-of-the-month. Lots of companies have employee-of-the-month programs, but now you have a way of doing your program that has massive impact. For example, don't just have one employee of the month, have several. Where does it say we only get to have one? Remember Scott Ostrander, general manager of the Resort and Club at CopperWynd? He decided to have two. He distinguished them as "front-of-the-house employee of the month" and "heart-of-the-house employee of the month."

3. Internal newsletters. Most companies have them. Begin using them for recognition instead of just education.

4. Press releases. I have a friend who says that if her company opens on time, she sends a press release, and if her employees weather the cold and flu season well, she sends a press release. Maybe that's overdoing it a bit, but think of the possibilities. When an employee goes to the industry national convention, send a press release announcing that she is going and another release when she returns announcing what she learned. The local paper and trade press will print it and your employees will cherish the recognition.

5. "Way-to-Go!" cards. In our world of email and other various forms of electronic communication, a handwritten note has more opportunity to stand out, get read and be remembered than ever before. As you notice the efforts and accomplishments worth recognizing, send a note directly to the employee thanking them. This may not be public, but it has every bit as much power as mentioning them in a speech. That you would take the time to sit down and write a note by hand speaks volumes about how you really feel about the employee or group and their performance and value to the company. So go ahead, make up some "Way-to-Go!" note cards and use them freely. But make sure you write them, not your secretary or assistant. That would be worse than not sending the card at all.

Take on involved recognition. It will alter your relationships; enhance morale, teamwork and service; and be modeled throughout your organization. What have you got to lose?

Never be afraid to try something new.
Remember, amateurs built the Ark;
professionals built the Titanic.
— Anonymous

Chapter 5

Habit #4: Looking to Greatness

Looking to greatness:
The habit of emphasizing strengths.

In sports, we hear debate after debate about the greatest team of all time, and the Boston Celtics are always included in the conversation. When I was growing up in southern New Hampshire in the 60s, following the Boston Celtics was my favorite pastime. And, believe it or not, it was the Celtics who first taught me about character, authenticity, attitude, contribution, commitment, determination, discipline, drive, embracing change, focus, integrity, motivation, creating possibility, risk, and emphasizing strengths.

Red Auerbach, then the head coach and general manager of the Celtics, was a master craftsman. He had an amazing talent for assembling groups of individual players who all knew the role they were supposed to play, were willing to play that role, and were passionately committed to one thing and one thing only — winning championships. During his tenure, Auerbach lead the Celtics to eight consecutive NBA Championship seasons and nine championships in all. He seemed to do this by focusing on the strengths of each player and allowing them to be the best they could be by looking to their greatness. Oh, sure, the Celtics had a few stars like Bill Russell, Bob Cousy and Sam Jones, but most of the players were role players. They were all good players, just not stars. Some of them had played for other teams with average results. But when they came together as members of the Boston Celtics, they became champions. All because Red Auerbach was willing to understand each player's strengths, and then relentlessly focused on those strengths. Auerbach never much cared that Bill Russell didn't score the most points, because he wasn't a scorer — he was a defensive and rebounding genius. Tom Sanders was perhaps the greatest defensive forward in the league during his time with the Celtics. Auerbach never tried to make Sanders into a flashy, high-scoring forward. He just wanted him to be the best defensive forward on the floor, every night. As he assembled championship team after championship team, Auerbach focused his attention on two things: First, it was imperative that every player was a team player. Second, he focused on their strengths and didn't spend a single minute trying to get his players to be something they were not. Red Auerbach was a Contagious Leader.

Contained Leaders have a habit of trying to move ahead by pushing people down; focusing on what's wrong, not what's right; pointing out weaknesses, not strengths. Sure, we can always do better and improve, but sometimes Contained Leaders focus so much attention on improving weaknesses that they don't spend nearly enough time fine-tuning strengths.

Let me give you another sports analogy: When I was a kid, I was a terrific baseball player. My dad always thought I could play in the majors as a catcher. Although I was right-handed, I always hit as a lefty. Don't ask me why or how it happened. I don't even remember. All I knew was that I could hit, consistently and with power, as a left-hander.

When I was in junior high school, my coach came up with this great idea that I should be a switch-hitter. That means I would hit left-handed when the pitcher was right-handed and right-handed when the pitcher was a lefty. They say it's easier to see the ball when you hit this way. At any rate, I was doing fine as a lefty, but the coach had me practice hitting right-handed every day. The end result was that I never did become much of a right-handed hitter, and my skills as a left-handed hitter diminished over time as I practiced to overcome a weakness rather than improving my strength.

Contagious Leaders take a completely different view. The goal of a Contagious Leader is to help each person become the best they can be, not to change them. For sure, the Contagious Leader is mindful of improving weak areas, but that's different from changing someone. The Contagious Leader takes time to really get to know each person — their strengths and their weaknesses — and then holds them accountable for being the best they can be. Looking to greatness involves four steps:

Step 1. Know your people.

As we said in Chapter 1, it's amazing how little most

Contained Leaders know about the personal lives of the people they work with. On the business side, most Contained Leaders don't have a clue as to the real strengths of most of the people reporting to them. Contagious Leaders know about their employees' education, technical skills, behavioral style, and values.

Knowing your people doesn't have to involve any uncomfortable or sophisticated systems. In many cases, you can just ask employees what they think their strengths are. Having real conversations with people can produce amazing results.

The educational and technical information is generally available on the person's resume. Study it, pay attention to it, and let it guide you. Generally speaking, the fact that your person studied English Literature as an undergraduate and graduate student may be a good indication that their strength lies in areas other than accounting or engineering. There are exceptions to every rule or generalization, of course, so you'll need to be careful. But get in the habit of talking to people — you'll be amazed what you learn.

As for behavior and values, I recommend that you use some form of profiles or assessment tools. My clients always benefit greatly from the use of these instruments. It is the only way I know to be clear on whether the employee and company or department are culturally compatible. Furthermore, I don't know of a better way to enhance interpersonal communication than using the results of our *Managing for Success*™ *Behavioral and Values Profiles.* I have even used these successfully in my own company to help drive interaction, creativity and communication. Through these profiles we learned that my strength is my ability to inspire others and conduct my affairs in a stable and dependable nature. My wife Beverly, on the other hand, is more of a driver, more results-oriented, more directed. Beverly is also more comfortable operating in a fast-paced environment with lots of change than I am.

For several years, we have used the *Managing for Success*™ system to help clients understand the strengths of individuals and teams. Our clients have successfully used these tools in several strategic areas:

- Improving hiring decisions by identifying people who are not just technically qualified but also, and perhaps more importantly, culturally compatible with the organization.

- Improving communications and leadership development by identifying and focusing on the behavioral strengths of individuals.

- Increasing sales productivity and customer care by helping individuals in these areas to communicate in a manner that is consistent with the customer/prospect behavioral style.

Using the *Managing for Success*™ profile is like playing with a two-piece puzzle. The first piece is behavior. The second piece is why we behave the way we do, what drives us. These profiles help companies select, manage, train, communicate with and empower the right people for each position. The profiles are administered online and take about 20 minutes to complete. The system then delivers, within three minutes, over 30 pages of information to help the individual and manager understand themselves and others at a level you never thought possible. The net result is a deep insight into how individuals behave and what drives their behavior.

By knowing each other better, my wife and I have been able to honor each other's strengths instead of working at defending our own ways of doing things. We will never, ever do things the same way. But when we focus on strengths and look to each other's greatness, we don't have to be right. We just have to be effective. These same benefits will accrue to any organization using these incredibly powerful tools.

Step 2. Integrate character.

Character will do more to alter the culture of your company than most anything else you can do. My friend Ian Percy, another wonderful speaker and author, once said to me that the next big trend in business will be ethics. That was before all the scandals and corporate malfeasances of 2002. Character and ethics are very close cousins. As Jean Paul Richter once observed, "Never does a man [or woman] portray his own character more vividly than in his manner of portraying another."

So character may well be the next big trend. We have evolved to a place where we need to remind ourselves that the only way to instill character in the workplace is to model it every day, in everything we do.

Step 3. Become a mentor.

Permission mentoring will be covered in Chapter 10, but let me go ahead and say that looking to greatness requires a different view of ourselves. We must see ourselves as mentors, not bosses. As Jack Welch put it, "We have to take out the boss element. We're going to win on our ideas, not by whips and chains." The Contained Leader tells individuals what to do and, more often than not, how to do it. The Contagious Leader creates an agreement on the desired outcome of a program or project and then supports the individual or team to accomplish the outcome, within the desired timeframe, using their strengths. There is no bossing involved. The Contagious Leader is a mentor, supporting the individual.

Step 4. Hold people accountable.

Looking to greatness may, at first glance, seem similar to the "open marriages" we read about in the 60s and early 70s when it was perfectly OK to do whatever you wanted as long as you were being true to yourself. The Contagious Leader does not abide by such a loose definition. Rather, they identify a person's strengths and then hold them accountable for delivering on that strength every day. Once you internalize this, it becomes clear that looking to greatness requires the Contagious Leader to hold people to high standards — standards the individual has set. Contagious Leadership is hard work. Letting people off the hook, lowering the high bar, and allowing people to perform to the lowest common denominator, is simple. It is also the way of Contained Leaders.

The benefits of looking to greatness are many. First, you'll experience a cultural shift as others model the habit. It is just more enjoyable focusing attention on what we are terrific at than on overcoming weaknesses. Try it with your family, particularly if you have children. For the most part, we have been incessantly reminding our kids of their weaknesses since birth. We put more energy into making them better math students than improving their natural strengths as artists. It is sad what this does. Ask a third grader to draw a picture of a purple elephant, and they'll sit right down and knock out the most amazing purple elephant you have ever seen. Ask them to do the same assignment as a fifth grader, and they will likely tell you that elephants are not purple. Ask them as a high-school freshman, and they'll say they are not much of an artist.

Looking to greatness also has a way of focusing attention on what is possible. Over time it builds confidence and trust and reduces conflict. We become accepting of the contribution that each team member is capable of making, and we slowly eliminate the need to be right. Championships are won by teams working together, not individuals dedicated to personal achievement. Championships are won, every day, when we look to greatness.

Chapter 6

Habit #5:
Vibrant Communication

Vibrant Communication:
The habit of effectively exchanging information, thoughts
and feelings that build unity and enhance productivity.

Communicating effectively has never been as difficult as it is today. Just getting through the noise is a challenge! Rebecca Z. Shafir, MACCC, author of *The Zen of Listening*, put it this way:

> *Welcome to the Age of Distraction! Never before has it been more difficult to get through an average day and feel a sense of accomplishment. According to Kirsten Downey Grimsley ("Message Overload Taking Toll on Workers,"* The Washington Post, *May 20, 1998), the average worker is interrupted six times every hour.*
>
> *David Shenk, author of* Data Smog, *reports that Americans were exposed to six times as many advertising messages in 1991 as they were in 1971. Shenk claims, "Information overload has replaced information scarcity as an important new emotional, social and political problem."*

Look at the dates of those statistics. I would guess it has gotten even worse since 1991 and 1998. Effective communication is difficult, but not as impossible as some Contained Leaders would have us believe.

Vibrant communication is exactly what the term implies: communication that cuts through the clutter because of its vibrancy. It is communication that occurs often, in various, perhaps even unexpected, forms to deliver compelling information. It is often the frequency and unexpected nature of the delivery mechanism that makes communication vibrant. Sending an email may be the most efficient delivery mechanism, but if you receive as many emails each day as I do, it can hardly be considered the most effective method.

Vibrant communication also implies that the vibrancy is far-reaching. Every member of the audience is given the information at the same time. That is not the way we generally communicate. Like the other habits, communication differs by leadership style.

The Contained Leader believes in keeping people guessing.

They only communicate what is absolutely necessary, only when it is absolutely necessary to do so, and only to people they feel have a real need to know. I'll never forget my very first day on the job as vice president of marketing for a major bank in Boston. It was in February 1978, and it was my first exposure to really bad communication.

This was not just any bank. This was history. This was the oldest mutual savings bank in the United States. It was so rich in tradition and history that many of the country's founding fathers had been customers. This bank was so old, so historic, that my office was actually a museum. No lie! I wasn't allowed to change a light bulb without someone else's approval.

As I walked across the equally famous and historic Boston Common for my first day on the job, my adrenaline was flowing at mach speed. The excitement and sense of anticipation was building with each step. I had grown up in the Boston area but had never worked in the city. Yet, here I was, 28 years old and vice president of marketing for one of the "big banks." This was an incredible opportunity.

I arrived at the bank and was escorted to the president's office. There, sitting around his enormous conference table, were all the other senior officers of the bank. I was impressed and delighted. How nice of them to gather to welcome me to the bank! What a great way to begin a new job!

Imagine my surprise and disappointment when I realized they were not there to welcome me or to discuss the bank's tradition and history.

On this wonderful first day in my exciting new job, my first meeting with the president and fellow senior officers was to discuss a little detail they had neglected to tell me about during the interviews. We were all there to strategically review how we were going to lay off 50 people that day.

You may not realize that banks didn't let people go without cause in 1978. The term "downsizing" would not be coined for another decade. Back then, working for a bank, particularly a mutual savings bank, was the equivalent of lifetime employment. It was like being a tenured teacher. A bank employee's future was totally secure and generally unaffected by performance — theirs or the bank's.

Nevertheless, this historic bank was about to do the unthinkable. And they had forgotten to tell me about it during the interview process. What a great example of Contained Leadership communication. Tell them only what they need to know and only when they have an absolute need to know it. There were two rather severe consequences of this communication failure. First, a new employee (me) was upset to learn this valuable piece of information after the fact. Second, the bank had not developed any plans for distributing this information to the public, the rest of the employees or the media. The following weeks were chaotic to say the least.

When the Charismatic Leader communicates, it is altogether different but no better. It is best described as manufactured inspiration, hype, and as little substance as possible. Just consider a politician being asked a question by a reporter. When is the last time you actually heard the politician answer the question? Generally, they dance around the issue and focus on some issue that is important to them but not necessarily relevant to the question. The answer is loaded with generalizations and clichés that, although difficult to argue with, never quite speak to the question.

The Contagious Leader has an entirely different style and level of commitment. He or she knows that nothing is more important to morale, performance and loyalty than open, honest communication that comes early and often, and is totally congruent with who they are and what they stand for.

Open and Honest Communication

Contagious Leaders fundamentally believe several things about people:
- They are trustworthy.

- They appreciate the truth.
- They can handle the truth.
- They prefer making decisions based on facts, not rumors.

How many times have you read a memo that indicated that so-and-so manager had decided to leave the company to pursue other business interests? How often do you think this is really accurate? More often than not, so-and-so manager has actually been fired, downsized or recruited away by one of the company's competitors. Why not say that? It is true that, in a few cases, it may not be in the best interest of the individual or company to tell the whole truth and nothing but the truth, so why not just say that so-and-so manager has left the company for personal reasons and we wish him well? Open and honest communication does not require us to divulge information that is personal or could negatively affect another person or company. In the case of so-and-so manager, it might have been that he and his manager didn't get along, or did not see eye to eye on strategic direction or mission or goals. The rest of the world does not need to know the details. It is none of their business. Most of us know this. The challenge is that, when confronted with a sticky situation, we generally give ourselves only two options: tell the whole truth or fabricate something that no one believes. We have grown so accustomed to these sleight-of-hand communications that we snicker and toss them aside. But the damage is done. Every time we communicate in a way that is not totally open and honest, we forfeit a little trust. It is like a bank account. Every time we do something well, we make a deposit into our employee trust account. When we do something poorly, it is a withdrawal. There is a compounding effect to these withdrawals: When we do finally communicate something as well as possible, there is a very strong chance that no one will believe it.

Here is the bottom line: Be open and honest. If you can't provide details, say so. "Harry has left the company. It was for personal reasons and we would be doing a disservice to Harry to say any more at this time. We hope you understand." Employees will appreciate your intentions.

Early Communication

I used to sit on the board of advisors of a company that was considering expansion. Rather than bring the board into the loop, management went to several local officials to "confidentially run the plans up the flagpole." Within an hour of the meeting, several of the board members had received telephone calls at home concerning changes at the company. The truth is that these "confidential conversations" were like talking out loud. You know, brainstorming. "If we did this or that or the other thing, how would you feel about it?"

Whether through local officials or the intercompany grapevine, news travels fast. And along the way it gets distorted. If your goal is to be a Contagious Leader and you are determined to build trust and unity among your employees and customers, open, honest and early communication is essential. There is nothing worse than reading about an event in the papers before the event has been announced.

Among other things, communicating early avoids mistakes, crises and rumors. Somehow the message that is leaked is always a bit inaccurate. It also reduces expenses in the long run, because cleaning up is always more expensive than doing the job right in the first place. More importantly, communicating early builds trust and loyalty. People feel involved. By having time to digest a situation, people can't help but feel that you actually care about them.

Frequent Communication

One of the first things I was taught in the advertising business was the concept of reach and frequency. The effectiveness of every communication dollar is a function of the message, the number of people in your target audience who are exposed to the message, and how often they are exposed to the message. Many years ago,

Apple Computer launched the Macintosh and defied many of the laws of reach and frequency. In a nutshell, Apple spent a bundle to produce one television commercial entitled "1984," and then ran it one time on one program, the Super Bowl. It was one of the most memorable and effective new product launches ever. They had a brilliantly created commercial that was exposed to millions and millions of people on the highest-rated TV program of the day. If it worked for Apple, why not for us, you ask?

First of all, most of what we communicate in business is not nearly as interesting or potentially exciting as an entirely new category of computers. As I said earlier, the production values are not even remotely similar. As I recall, Apple spent in excess of $1 million to just produce this 60-second movie. Finally, one of the laws of nature seems to be that there is an exception to every law. Apple's Macintosh was the exception.

For communication to be truly effective, it has to have frequency. Jack Welch was a master at frequent vivid communication. He would settle on a particular initiative for the company and then speak about it at every opportunity. It would seem as though this initiative was the only thing this giant organization cared about. Welch knew that people need to hear from Contagious Leaders early and often if they are expected to know that you truly are committed to keeping them informed.

Congruent Communication

There is nothing worse than saying one thing and doing another. Consider the following:

- In your annual report, the CEO renews the company's commitment to long-term results, investing in the future, and no longer allowing short-term results to dictate decision-making. Shortly thereafter, the company announces it is reducing the labor force by 20% because the most recent quarter's results were disappointing. How are the employees, customers or market analysts supposed to interpret that?

- A company announces a price increase because the cost of doing business has risen, but the CEO is awarded a huge bonus, despite the fact that the company's performance has been well below market expectation.

- The company consistently proclaims, as a matter of policy, its commitment to family values, yet your boss consistently asks you to work overtime and miss dinner with your family.

- The vice president of sales announces a tightening of the belt on client entertainment and reinforces the point by taking a small group on a golf boondoggle to the Bahamas.

If you haven't already figured it out, I have great admiration for Jack Welch's Contagious Leadership style. When he first took over as chairman and CEO of GE, he asked the HR people, who were responsible for administering the annual employee opinion survey, to add a question. It went something like this: "Is the GE that you work for the same GE that you read about in our annual report and marketing literature?" That is a wonderful example of a Contagious Leader who was concerned about being congruent.

In Chapter 1, I said that to catch the Contagious Leadership fever, we have to *be* Contagious Leaders. I never said it would be easy, just powerfully effective. As I created the chapter titles for this book, I chose each word carefully. The adjective *vibrant* was no exception. Webster defines *vibrant* as "pulsating with life, vigor or activity."

If nothing else, communication is an active, pulsating and vigorous process. Contagious Leaders have an exceptional respect and admiration for that process and the challenges to which communication gives birth. "The habit of effectively exchanging information, thoughts and feelings that build unity and enhance productivity" can never be taken lightly or treated passively. It is an active process, an all-inclusive process. Contagious Leaders insist on it also being open, honest, early, frequent and congruent.

Chapter 7

Habit #6: Unobstructed Vision

Unobstructed Vision: *The habit of focusing attention on a clear and sensory-rich picture of the desired result.*

To see or not to see, that is the challenge. Contained Leaders have no vision of their own. They are short-term implementers, and their vision is always of what *they* should do. Theirs is a company, department or regional vision that is someone else's creation. Contained Leaders always have a freshly updated resume in their computer and a willingness to take advantage of the next great opportunity that comes their way.

Contagious Leaders hold three essential components of vision in high regard: clarity, commitment and communication. Their vision belongs to *them*. Even if the vision began as the company's or department's, the Contagious Leader has found a way to make it theirs. The vision is clear and most certainly pertains to what is possible. Because it is their creation, Contagious Leaders are firmly committed to their vision, maintaining focus and rarely allowing distractions. Contagious Leaders believe that sharing their vision publicly and declaring their intentions serves to intensify clarity and commitment.

Clarity

In Chapter 3, we said that Contagious Leaders practice the habit of making responsible choices about "how" we do things, not just "what" we do. Their ability to accomplish this is completely a function of the Contagious Leader's clarity of both.

The Contained Leader places nearly all of their attention on the "what" — what she or he, the department, region or company is supposed to do. Increasing sales, improving efficiency, reducing expenses, training more people, getting the direct mail program completed, minimizing customer complaints, meeting the deadline for the new advertising campaign, creating a new brochure, emailing the press release about the CEO's anniversary party, networking with other industry leaders, and publishing articles for the industry trade press are all examples of "what." The list can be endless and will keep the Contained Leaders very, very busy. Sadly, Contained Leaders have little or no clarity about the "how" of these activities. Character never enters their consideration set. Qualities like attitude, authenticity, contribution, commitment, determination, discipline, drive, focus, integrity, motivation, creating possibility, and risk never enter the picture. Just "getting the job done" is their reason for being; getting it done in the most expedient way. "How" the job gets done is not only a secondary consideration, it is rarely considered at all.

Are Contained Leaders bad? Not at all! Most are a product of family, school and work environments that exclusively focused on the "what." They have succeeded by developing a one-dimensional vision. Fortunately, I got caught with this one-dimensional vision early on and learned a valuable lesson. In was in my final semester in college, and I had taken one of those "gut courses." You know the one — the easy course, the sure thing, the course that requires very little effort for a very big return. In this case, the return was a passing grade. Since the course was offered as a pass/fail, all I wanted was a passing grade. It was not a course I needed to fulfill my major requirements. It was not a course I would ever use to advance my business career. This was a course in weather. You know, cumulus and nimbus clouds and such. As far as I was concerned, all I needed to know about weather could be learned by looking out the window. Little did I know that my professor was a Contagious Leader. "How" these passing grades were achieved mattered to him.

My final semester in college was the spring of 1975. The economy was just a bit shaky, and many of my classmates were concerned about getting jobs. As I was married and considerably older than most of the other students, my focus at the time was on getting a great job. I spent most of my final semester sending out resumés, going on job interviews, and following up on possible leads. I learned that looking for a job could be a full-time job. Unfortunately, I had two other paying jobs, so something had to give. What gave was the weather. I showed up for tests and nothing else. This, after all, was a "gut" course. The professor was sure to understand. WRONG!

To this professor, "how" was just as important as "what." It was important that each student show up and make an effort. He never asked anyone to go on to be a weather expert, just to show up and have a little respect for him, his material and his efforts. I passed the course, but only after begging the professor. It was a great lesson about character and clarity.

Commitment

Contained Leaders *have* to make commitments. Contagious Leaders *get* to. It is a choice, not a requirement. Whether the vision is theirs or they have taken ownership of the company's or department's vision, the Contagious Leader makes a conscious choice to be committed to seeing the vision through.

The Contained Leader also makes a conscious choice. It is a choice to be somewhat committed to the vision. Occasionally it is a choice to be committed to themselves and not the vision. That's why Contained Leaders always have an updated resumé handy. They have a first-name relationship with the best head hunters and they are always in play and available to discuss new opportunities. Don't misunderstand. Contagious Leaders do not have their heads in the sand. It's not like they never consider good opportunities. They are not so committed that they would willingly go down with the ship. Quite the contrary, in fact. Contagious Leaders are more in demand than Contained Leaders. This is due in part to their ability and willingness to develop and commit to a clear, unobstructed vision.

Communication

As we established in Chapter 6, Contagious Leaders have a fundamental belief that employee and customer attitudes and behavior are largely the by-product of communication. When we feel involved, understand the direction, and realize the effort and sometimes even sacrifices we are being asked to make, we make better choices. From better, more informed choices come durable commitments, unyielding determination and resolute discipline. Lee Iacocca, former chairman of Chrysler and a Contagious Leader in many ways, had such a belief system. His vision of a healthy and prosperous Chrysler was so convincing that he enrolled Congress, the unions, the factory workers, administrative personnel and management in the great "Chrysler Bail-Out" program. Perhaps even more notable, he enrolled the public in his vision so strongly that millions not only agreed with the bail-out, but began to believe in the Chrysler product again. This may actually go down in history as the most extraordinary business turnaround in history. This dramatic turnaround occurred because one man had a clarity of vision, an unshakable commitment, and an ardent belief that the world would choose to be on Chrysler's side after being presented with and considering the facts. Lee Iacocca had unobstructed vision.

The Benefits of an Unobstructed Vision

Bill J. Bonnstetter, president and CEO of Target Training International, Ltd., in Scottsdale, Arizona, and coauthor of *The Universal Language, DISC*, said, "Every interaction you have with a person either increases or decreases your endorsement. Human performance is directly proportional to endorsement." We could substitute "credibility" or "influence" for "endorsement," but I rather like Bill's choice of words. He further believes that endorsement is gained from position, appearance and beliefs. Endorsement gained from position or appearance can be somewhat fleeting, but endorsement gained from beliefs will stand on firm ground. As for endorsement gained from beliefs, Bonnstetter says, "A person who does what they say and says what they do will develop greater endorsement than a person who is wishy-washy in their actions."

Endorsement is an enormous benefit to having an unobstructed vision. The strength of a Contagious Leader comes from the ability to create endorsement. Through the vision and an unrelenting dedication to painting it with brilliant colors, every person touched by the vision has the ability to make an informed choice as to whether it is a vision they will buy into. Not every person will adopt the vision, but those who do are in for the duration. By gaining this level of endorsement, a Contagious Leader opens the possibility of developing other Contagious Leaders rather than attracting a group of mindless followers who show up every day because the boss said they had to. Endorsement breeds modeling that further generates a culture built around clarity, commitment and communication.

Imagine you and every person in your company being so enthusiastic about your jobs and your futures that you go to bed each night with the feeling that there just wasn't enough time in the day to do all the things you wanted to do. Imagine that enthusiasm. Imagine the results it would produce, the spirit, the determination, the productivity. How would you like to experience this every day? How would you like to have every employee experience this every day?

Go create an unobstructed vision.

Developing Your Unobstructed Vision

Developing an unobstructed vision involves four steps:
1. Decide
2. Practice
3. Develop passion
4. Make it your own

Step 1. Decide to be a Contagious Leader.

It is really that simple, just a decision. It is amazing but true that a decision has preceded every great act, every great effort. Mohammed Ali declared, "I am the greatest" long before he was recognized as a truly great heavyweight boxing champion. Ted Turner was ridiculed for having the temerity to even think there could be a fourth major television network, but he declared it so, long before it came to pass. A friend told me a wonderful story about Bette Midler, a huge recording star, as well as a star of stage and movies. In the mid-sixties, my friend was a talk show host for WNEW radio in New York. At the time, WNEW had its studio on the street level of the Empire State Building. They had a large picture window on the street level so passersby could watch the radio program on their way to work. Early every morning for a month or so, this young woman came by the studio. She was dressed in the garb of the day: hip-hugger, bell-bottom jeans with an American flag stitched to her behind, a tie-died shirt, hoop earrings, platform shoes and an Army backpack instead of a purse. She would stand in front of the picture window and look inside until the producer or host noticed her. Then, as if on cue, she would begin to jump in the air, waving her hands and occasionally pounding on the window while screaming at the top of her lungs, "Interview me, interview me, I'm gonna be a star!" This "crazy lady," as they referred to her, was a novelty at first, but she quickly became a nuisance. How were they to know that this "crazy lady" would soon be known as the Divine Miss M? Bette Midler, like Mohammed Ali, Ted Turner and countless others, had made a decision to be great. Greatness, Contagious Leadership and unob-structed vision do not always follow as quickly from the decision to the result as it did in these cases, but there is little doubt that they begin with a decision.

Step 2: Practice the habits and qualities outlined in this book.

Great leaders always model other great leaders. Why reinvent the wheel? Do, every day, what Contagious Leaders do, and the product of your efforts is assured.

Step 3: Decide whether the vision of your company, department or region is one you can passionately adopt.

Without passion, your chances of developing an unobstructed vision will be severely limited. Remember, this is a passion for both the "what" and the "how." You'll have to ask yourself if you can fervently support both "what" you'll be doing and "how" you are expected to deliver the results. If you don't have this passion, I suggest you do yourself and your employer a favor — go find a vision you can passionately and intensely support. You are not doing yourself or your company any good by going through the motions every day. This very morning, I watched an interview with Jack Welch about hiring and developing leaders. He was asked what he looked for in people. He said he didn't care much about the person's resume or background. Sure, these were important, but more important was whether the candidate had any passion about succeeding, learning and developing others. Welch wanted to know if there was anything a person was passionate about, what it was, and whether he or she could find that opportunity at GE. Welch said the last thing he wanted was a qualified candidate who sat back and complained that "the people at the top" were idiots and didn't know how to run a company.

If that sounds like you, how much fun are you having at work every day with this attitude? Remember, you either "get to" or you "have to." The choice is yours. Without passion, you'll never develop an unobstructed vision, and without an unobstructed vision, your ability to create an environment of Contagious Leadership will be seriously challenged.

Step 4: Make it your own.
This isn't complicated, but it's not easy either. Knowing your job description and responsibilities relative to the company, department or regional vision, you will begin to think in terms of the end result. What will it look like when this vision of yours is accomplished? What will sales be? What will product quality be? What will customer service, employee retention rates, profitability, return of investment and return on equity be? How much will you

be earning? What will your title be? Where will you live — what city, town, street and house? Begin to develop a crystal-clear vision of these and any other elements that are pertinent to accomplishing your vision. The critical thing to remember in Step 4 is to focus on the end result.

Joelle Hadley has a terrific story about developing an unobstructed vision. She recently stepped down as publisher of *The Business Journal of Phoenix* to launch her own training business. We had lunch and she shared her story. At the age of 22, Joelle graduated from college and went to work in advertising sales for *The Business Journal of Kansas*. She remembers very clearly saying to herself that she wanted an annual salary of $100,000 by the time she was 30 years old. She did not obsess over this, but she did have clarity about it and she was totally committed and passionate. She made the decision, she practiced the habits and qualities of a Contagious Leader, she had passion, and she made it her own. Joelle reminded herself every day, week, month and year that her vision was to earn $100,000. Joelle is a person of very deep convictions and character, so the "how" was very important to her. As for the "what," she was terrific at advertising sales and advanced quickly. In just a couple of years, she was promoted to advertising director for *The Business Journal of Phoenix* and later, at the age of 28, was named publisher. A couple of years later, she received her annual raise and bonus. Surprise, surprise! Adding the raise and bonus to her current salary totaled exactly $100,000. Ah, the power of an unobstructed vision!

Chapter 8

Habit #7: Touching Lives

Touching lives: The habit of truly knowing your most valuable assets — people.

Business is up close and personal. Always has been, always will be. Despite all the advances in technology — all the faster, better, sleeker ways of doing tasks with PDAs, wireless devices, laptops and on-the-spot Internet-communication systems — people are still the most important asset in any company. Always have been, always will be.

Contained Leaders don't agree with the above. Ask a Contained Leader the name of her secretary's children or where his vice president of marketing lives, or what the VP of IT's favorite pastime is, and you'll get a blank stare. We have all seen that look before. We sometimes confuse it to mean, "Gee, I don't know the answer," when it really means, "Who cares and why would you be asking me such a dumb question anyway?" Contained Leaders are not the least bit interested in touching lives — just in making numbers, getting results, building a strong and compelling portfolio of success that they can auction to the highest bidder. Little do they know that if they touched a few lives, their portfolio might have a value beyond anything they could have imagined.

The great Dr. Wayne Dyer makes a brilliant distinction between believing and knowing. He reminds us that when we go swimming or riding a bike, we don't just *believe* we can do it. We *know* we can. Contagious Leaders *know* their business is about touching lives. Regardless of the nature of their business, it is always about people — satisfying people, influencing people, mentoring people, inspiring people. Contagious Leaders have a deep knowing that performance comes from people — product-development people who designed the product that is made by manufacturing people and sold by salespeople who sell to customer people who pay money for the product. That money is processed by financial people to provide shareholder value and a return on investment for the people who believed enough in the people running the company to invest the money they earned doing one of these functions somewhere else.

Contagious Leaders are committed to touching as many lives

as possible. Not because it is a good business decision, but because it is the right thing to do, and doing the right thing defines the Contagious Leader. It reminds me of another story that I first heard from Dr. Wayne Dyer:

It seems there was a village that was ruled by a mad and ruthless king. He built a prison on the outskirts of the village into which he had wrongly placed many of the villagers. Left in the village were the elderly, children and four wise and kind human beings.

Stories of the poor conditions in the prison and how the prisoners were mistreated reached the four wise and kind human beings. The first three of these wise and kind human beings were men of great wealth and holdings. The king allowed them to provide clothing, linens, blankets, bedding and crops to feed the starving prisoners. The fourth wise and kind human had no wealth, no clothes, no bedding, and no crops to give. One night as she lay in her bed considering how she might best serve the entire village, she had a vision in which she discovered where the keys to the prison were hidden. Late the next night, she unlocked the prison gates, setting the prisoners free to return to their families.

This story illustrates how we often take the easy road in our attempts to create the appearance of touching lives. The first three wise and kind men used only a tiny portion of their vast fortunes to make the suffering prisoners more comfortable. The woman risked her very life to free the prisoners, return them to their families, and eliminate the suffering for all. That is touching lives.

Up Close and Personal

My wife Beverly has a very dear friend, David Downs, whose first job out of college was to travel throughout Europe and interview athletes for the Olympic Games. This was the beginning of the now-famous "Up Close and Personal" segments from *ABC Sports* that millions of us have so enjoyed throughout the years. The idea was simply brilliant. By getting to know the athletes, barriers were removed. The better we got to know the trials and tribulations, the efforts, the accomplishments, the failures and the hurdles of each athlete, the more connected we became. We learned to admire, perhaps even like, the athletes, regardless of their country or political beliefs. It was like having a family member or friend in the Olympics. The better we knew the athletes, the more we watched the games. The more we watched, the more often we were exposed to commercials. With improvement in audience delivery and reach and frequency came added revenue for the network. Everyone was a winner: the viewing audience, the advertisers, the network. But that was not necessarily the goal. Someone once told me that Roone Arledge, then the president of *ABC Sports*, just thought the viewing audience would enjoy the Games more if they knew the athletes better.

What a concept! Do you think it might apply to our companies? Do you think people who know one another better might enjoy working together? The fact is that we, too, can break down barriers, just like *ABC Sports*, by getting to know people better. We can build trust and confidence as well. And with the trust, confidence and removal of barriers comes a commitment to possibility that most companies only dream about.

Getting To Know You,
Getting To Know All About You

Unfortunately, there are some issues we need to be aware of regarding touching lives. The first is that there are certain legal issues that your manager of HR will have to brief you about. Asking certain questions in an effort to get to know an individual better can actually get us in trouble. So be careful and check with HR. Then there are just two common-sense steps you'll need to follow.

Step 1. Slow Down!

Beverly has an interesting way of looking at this process. She says that getting acquainted with employees is like dating. Once we make the decision to be a Contagious Leader, we can be in such a rush that we scare the employees away. When Beverly and I started our first business together, she was constantly reminding me that men and women usually prefer the hard-to-get types. Even as dating teenagers, we fell victim to the ones who didn't show that they liked us very much. The more aloof they were, the harder we tried to convince them to like us. Getting acquainted with employees and/or customers is somewhat the same. The process needs time to be nurtured and grow. You are not going to decide to be a Contagious Leader on Sunday and have the Touching Lives chapter handled by Tuesday.

First of all, keep in mind that, for many of us, it was only yesterday that we had very little interest in getting to know the people we work with. Now, as if we suddenly saw the "biggest Contagious Leader of all" sitting in a burning bush, we want to know everyone, and right now. We begin to force ourselves on the employees. We think they will like the fact that we are open to building a truly long-term relationship when, in fact, we scare the heck out of them. Ask yourself, wouldn't that scare you away? Slow down!

Step 2. Remember that less is more!

Have you ever noticed that when a prospect creates even the slightest impression that they are interested in a product or service, the sales and marketing folks tend to back a 40-foot trailer up to their home or office and start unloading facts? We think, the more the better: "If I send Harry a presentation with all the information, he is more likely to buy." The reality is that Harry takes one look at the three-inch folder of charts, graphs, technical explanations, marketing mumbo-jumbo and expert testimonials from the likes of "AL in Florida" and immediately shuts down. It is true that some individuals or customers may want this depth of information. But, as we learn from the behavioral profiles we use with our clients, many people need to build a relationship before we offer specifics. Less is *always* more. The job of a Contagious Leader is to make people want to give and receive more information.

To really get acquainted, we need to build trust, and that takes time. Trust is just not something we can demand. We can't send an email declaring that we are trustworthy, genuinely care about every person on the planet, and consequently expect every employee to "come clean" and tell us all the good stuff so we can satisfy our burning desire to prove to the boss that we did everything we were told to do in the book they suggested we read.

There is an old saying: "People don't care what you know until they know you care." Contagious Leaders naturally attract people by honestly caring about others. They are like magnets. People just know that Contagious Leaders care about others and they truly wish to make a difference and do whatever they can to help as many people as possible get what they want. Contagious Leaders make a habit of touching lives.

Nido Qubein, CSP, CPAE, my mentor and friend, calls this relational capital. Our relationships with employees, customers and prospects are an asset just like plant, equipment, inventory and good will. Relational capital is all about who you know and who knows you. Nido has taught me that the value of relational capital is not determined by whether we know someone's name, but whether we know them well and they know us well. He has dedicated his entire business career to touching lives. Nido is constantly on the lookout for ways to make a difference in the lives of people he meets. He'll read an article or a book and think, "Who do I know who might benefit from this?" Then he will send those individuals the article or book. Here's the brilliant part: Nido has invested considerable time and energy getting to know people, at a deep level, so he knows whether the book or article would be meaningful. And, although he is the recipient of considerable payback from this approach, that's not why he does it. Nido Qubein cares about people — he cares about making a difference to others. That's why he does it. His coaching has taught me to nurture and develop my relational capital every day. There is nothing more important for me to do in the course of my day.

Contagious Leaders place a high value on nurturing their relational capital. They work it daily. We are all time-pressured, and Contained Leaders simply cannot spare a moment with employees. Contagious Leaders know that, time-pressured or not, spending time to get closer with employees is exactly what they need to be doing.

You are probably sick of hearing my Jack Welch stories, but I find them fascinating and instructive. Recently I met a man named Steve in my hometown of Fountain Hills, Arizona. He had just moved here from Atlanta. He mentioned that he had worked for GE and told me a story that illustrated the point of getting to know employees. He attended a GE meeting some years ago that Mr. Welch also attended. Steve had been briefly introduced to Welch 12 years earlier but had not been in his company since then. As Welch moved around the room, he made eye contact with Steve and came over to him. He said "Hi, Steve, how are you? It has been a long time! How is your wife Barbara and how is it going in the XX division in Atlanta?" Steve was blown away. Prior to that moment, he would have bet money that Jack Welch would not remember him, let alone the name of his wife or the division for which he worked. But Jack Welch was and will always be a Contagious Leader. He made it his business to know his people. Steve felt important to GE and to Mr. Welch. How many times do you figure Steve may have told that story? Is it possible that he learned anything from it? Do you think perhaps he passed this on to some of his direct reports? How do you think this made them feel about their company?

Touching lives can pay huge dividends to a company, region, department or work group. Contagious Leaders know this but, more importantly, they know that making a difference for others is just the right thing to do.

Chapter 9

Habit #8:
A Passionate Stand

A passionate stand:
The habit of being fully expressed.

The world will belong to passionate, driven leaders —
people who not only have enormous amounts of energy
but who can energize those whom they lead.

— Jack Welch
Former Chairman & CEO,
General Electric Company

Contained Leaders are not passionate. They are controlled in everything they do. When they do get excited, it is usually contrived and created for the express purpose of attempting to motivate others. It is short-lived, lasting just long enough for the one speech, one meeting, or one big event, and then it's back to being in control.

Contagious Leaders are always passionate, but not necessarily in a cheerleader sort of way. Contagious Leaders live their entire life — their business life, personal life, family life and community life — out on what I call the skinny part of the branches.

Contained Leaders spend their lives hugging the trunk of the tree. At an early age, they climbed up into the tree of life. In striving for safety and comfort, they migrated to the strongest part of the tree — the trunk — and settled there. The trunk of the tree is where they think their business and their lives are safe and secure. They lean against the trunk of the tree, folding their arms around it. They steady themselves from the elements of life. The tree holds them up and does most of the work. They don't make the calls on new prospects that they need to make. They don't network with those who have gone before them to learn what it takes to get to the top. They make recommendations to their clients that are in their best interest, not the client's. They avoid getting to know the people they work with, they avoid touching lives. They offer their families the leftovers — the time left over at the end of a busy day. They hide from their families under the big branches while they hug the trunk of the tree.

The truth is that it's more fun out on the branches where we have to do all the work. Where we don't have anyone or anything holding us up. Sure it's risky! But it's also exhilarating being out on the skinny part of the branches. Out there, we feel a little unsteady, always a little bit at risk. But only from there can we experience the adrenaline rush we talked about in Chapter 3. Only from out there can we experience that feeling of being exhilarated and terrified at exactly the same moment.

If you want to catch a glimpse of life on the skinny part of the branches, watch your kids at play. They are afraid of nothing; they try everything, frequently, without ever considering the consequences. They are unencumbered by reasonableness.

Contained Leaders convince themselves that life is safe back near the trunk of the tree where they are protected from the elements. The "big branches" are above them. When it rains, they don't get quite so wet. When it is windy, their hair doesn't get quite so messed up. In frigid weather, they don't get quite so cold. But they never feel energized and exhilarated either.

And you know what? Hugging the trunk of the tree doesn't mean we never fall. Of course we do; life consists of falls. Life on the skinny part of the branches may mean you risk falling a few more times, but that's the good news. You'll have more fun before, during and after the fall and, after all, what would life be like if we couldn't compare our successes with our failures?

Creating Your Passionate Stand

Since most of us have spent our entire adult lives hugging the trunk of the tree, we want to be prudent here. We don't want to move from the trunk to the branches in one big superman-type leap. If we do, we're likely to miss the branch completely.

We need to take one tiny step at a time, holding on with both arms while we try something new. Then, as we feel more comfortable in this foreign territory, we ease our feet out away from the trunk while holding on with both hands. Then we move away, holding on with just our fingertips. And then finally with no hands, we inch our way out to the middle of the branches. Building confidence as we go farther, we finally get to the end — to the skinny branches.

At first, dreams seem impossible, then improbable,
and eventually inevitable.
— Christopher Reeve, Actor

Creating your passionate stand involves a number of steps:

Step 1. Decide what you are passionate about.

This may seem humorous, but many of us spend our days in activities that simply do not move us. What moves you? What is it about your job that moves you, that gets you really excited? What do you really enjoy doing in your spare time? What family activities or community projects make the hair stand up on the back of your neck? Make a list of these activities. Categorize and prioritize them so you can gain some clarity about your passions.

Step 2. Analyze Step 1.

Calculate how much of your time is spent in the activities you are passionate about. You'll be amazed! No wonder you're not feeling passionate. You love selling, but you spend only 5% of your time in the selling process and 95% doing tedious paperwork.

Step 3. Pick one passion.

Pick one passion from any of the categories. It doesn't really matter what you pick. This is all about practice. I want you to improve the equation by 25%. For example, let's say you are in sales and love the process, but only 20% of your time is spent prospecting — the part you love most. So, for the next week, I want you to increase that to at least 25%. In this case, it means you would spend 25% of your time prospecting in the next week. Then increase it again for the following week.

You can do this with any or all of your passion priorities. If you love attending your child's soccer games but spend only 5% of your time doing so, then make a plan for increasing it by 5% next week. You can find an extra hour and 15 minutes for something as important as this passion, can't you?

This isn't about time management, just practicing our priorities, especially the ones we are passionate about. It is focusing our attention on getting out to the skinny part of the branches. When we say, "I can't go to the soccer match for an extra 75 minutes because I'm just too darn busy," we are being a Contained Leader by allowing circumstances to be in control rather than setting priorities around our passion. Remember, being a Contagious Leader by being passionate in everything we do is a decision. If family is your passion, you have to make the decision to focus on that passion by structuring the rest of your life around it. Just try it for one week. Try setting your priorities and devoting most of your time, focus and energy to your passion without sacrificing your performance or productivity in other areas of your life. It's a challenge but that's what being out on the skinny part of the branches is all about.

Step 4. Pick up the pace.

Keith Harrell offers a suggestion about attitude that works for passion as well. Decide right now that, for the next week, you will do everything 25% better, faster, greater. You will walk 25% longer, talk 25% faster, commit to getting work completed in 25% less time, spend 25% more time with family and friends, spend 25% more time doing the important aspect of your job, and giving 25% more to your community or church. See what happens when you just practice picking up the pace.

The Contagious Leader takes a passionate stand by practicing the habit of being fully expressed. We just described a fully expressed individual as a person who engages in every aspect of their lives. They take on more, accomplish more, enjoy more and contribute more by being fully expressed. It is a decision! Try it!

Step 5. Take a passionate stand.

My wife Beverly has always enjoyed the theater. When she lived in Portsmouth, New Hampshire, many years ago, she was involved in the Theatre by the Sea. Recently she began to involve herself in our community theater in Fountain Hills, Arizona. It is a great organization that has been around for 17 years or so and produces wonderful entertainment year in and year out. Because Beverly is a Contagious Leader, she was noticed right away. In a matter of weeks, she was asked to serve as president of the Fountain Hills Community Theater Friends Group. The mission of the Friends Group is to gain more community involvement. Beverly decided to take it on in a big way — her typically unreasonable way.

In the past, the Friends Group consisted of a few friends who volunteered to help out. Beverly had a much larger vision. Her first vision was the theater not having to rely on the town for any funding. If it came, great, but they were just fine without it. Her second vision was that this fabulous organization and wonderful entertainment would no longer be the best-kept secret in town. Beverly took a very big stand. The group announced that anyone could be a "friend" for just $10. Then they announced that there would be a kick-off party at the home of the president and founder on a Sunday afternoon in August. Do you have any idea how hot it can get in Arizona in August? The day came and it was nearly 108 degrees. About 100 people attended the party, including the mayor, most of the town council members, and the executive director and president of the Chamber of Commerce. When it came time for Beverly to make a few comments, she took an even bigger stand. She publicly declared that there would be 500 members of the Fountain Hills Community Theater Friends Group by the end of September, and 4000 by the end of the year. WOW!

Beverly freely admits that she had been excited about the theater all along. When she took a passionate stand and went public with it, her excitement turned to passion. She is unstoppable.

Beverly is accustomed to doing this. She does it all the time. When our business, or a project she is working on, needs some energy, she takes a passionate stand. She did it with this book. I had returned from the National Speakers Association annual convention where I attended a workshop about getting published. The workshop leader suggested that the standard way of writing a

book was a terrifying labor. Because of our very busy travel sched-
ules, most speakers write when time permits — on airplanes, in
hotel rooms, on Saturday mornings when they are in town. It
works, but can take forever and can be frustrating and exhausting.
The workshop leader offered an alternative: write an entire book
in two weekends. I had my doubts that this could ever be accomplished. However, when Beverly heard this, she insisted that we
take it on with passion. So, after the research was completed, we
picked two weekends for the project — one to outline this book
and one to write it. Guess what? It happened! Well, nearly
happened. On Sunday afternoon of the second weekend, the first
draft of this book was 90% completed.

What will you take a passionate stand for? Whatever it is, I
promise that it will alter your life in every way. The spillover is
incredible. Make sure you involve as many of your senses as
possible. See it, feel it, touch it, smell it, hear it as often as you can.
And make sure you are unreasonable. When someone says you
can't do something, or suggests a project that can't be accomplished in the time frame you initially set out, be unreasonable.
Play for high stakes, play full out! You may not always hit your
goal, but you will always come closer to doing so than if you had
played in a more reasonable way.

Step 6. Check your support system.

Being passionate about your family, job, project or any other
venture requires a supportive environment. So the first thing to do
is involve everyone around you. Ask them to make a commitment
to help you accomplish your passionate stand. Involve them early
so there are no surprises. Don't just expect the kids to understand
why you are working late every night. Sit them down and ask
for their help and support. The project will not take forever;
you won't be working late for the rest of their lives. Explain it to
them ahead of time. Remember, Contagious Leaders practice
vibrant communications.

The same is true with your company. You'll need to assess whom you can count on to support you and the company in this passionate stand. It will be good to know who will be with you, who will be on the fence, and who will not support you at all.

Taking a passionate stand can revitalize you, and it can become habit-forming. Once you start doing 25% more, once you practice being unreasonable, you'll be amazed how easy it is to keep it up.

Chapter 10
Habit #9: Permission Mentoring

Permission mentoring: *The habit of ripening aspiring Contagious Leaders.*

The Demise of the Dictator

In 1989, Jack Welch, once called "Neutron Jack" for his willingness to let people go, initiated a program called "Work-Out" in an effort to capture the great ideas of workers, engage their minds, and clean up GE by getting rid of all the bureaucratic nonsense that had slowed the company down for years. The GE Work-Out program is actually a great case for transforming Contained Leadership to Contagious Leadership, and was a very important element in GE's transforming itself into perhaps the world's greatest leadership factory.

Contained Leaders don't mentor; they tell, they direct, they demand and they dictate, but they never, ever mentor. Their communication style is very direct, very one-dimensional. They speak, we listen; they tell, we do! It is very focused on the "what" rather than the "how." As a result, the Contained Leader has become quite good at creating followers but not more leaders.

The challenge with creating followers is that they follow. All too often they follow mindlessly. They offer no suggestions, provide no feedback, develop no creative alternatives, don't think or act outside the box, don't create possibility, and don't take any risks. They just follow! Over the past 20 or so years, I have learned that all employees, especially those responsible for actually doing a particular job, may have some very good thoughts on how to do the job better. But it takes a Contagious Leader to first ask for suggestions, really listen to them when they are given, provide feedback on the idea quickly, and finally implement the approved ideas in a timely fashion.

At this point, we need to get one thing straight. In every organization, business, church, school and family, there are workers, managers, Contained Leaders and Contagious Leaders. The category each person falls into is largely a matter of choice. Not every worker wants to be a manager, not every manager wants to be a leader, and not every Contained Leader wants to be Contagious. In some cases, it is a matter of talent, but these cases are not nearly as frequent as we may think. In fact, in his book, *Primal Leadership*, Daniel Goleman says that talent is 10% cognitive skills (technical training) and 90% emotional intelligence (empathy, collaboration, resonance, communication). The more advanced our society and businesses become, the more individuals are making choices that reflect lifestyle preferences over career.

My daughter Kate graduated from college a year or so ago. Kate has tremendous qualities, but the one I most admire and am most proud of is her clear understanding of herself. She values family first and, frankly, isn't looking for a high-flying, rock-em-sock-em career. She wants to work in an energizing environment that allows her to express her boundless creative talents while contributing through her highly-developed natural ability to influence and relate to others. She also wants a steady environment, not some 1000-miles-an-hour, 24-hours-a-day, 7-days-a-week program like I was in at the same age. Kate is making choices that are right for her, as are many employees. Not everyone wants to move on to a leadership position, and fewer still are honestly looking to be Contagious Leaders. This is all the more reason for practicing permission mentoring. Remember that this term means to ripen aspiring Contagious Leaders. An attempt to mentor someone with no intention of taking on a leadership position would not only be a waste of valuable time, it would ultimately annoy the employee. In the end, we would run the risk of losing a wonderfully productive person because we wanted them to be something or someone they had no interest in being.

Contagious Leaders fundamentally believe that a very big part of their job is to develop future Contagious Leaders. They see themselves as part coach, part player and part general manager. As the general manager, they make decisions about team makeup. Remember Red Auerbach of the Boston Celtics? When he traded for Willie Nauls, the fans said, "Great, but who is Willie Nauls?" It turned out that Nauls was a great role player. He was a wonderful scorer who could come off the bench with a moment's notice and light up the team. All general managers sometimes have to make these decisions without counseling the rest of the team. As coach, Contagious Leaders see themselves as a guide rather than a task master. She asks but does not tell; he requests rather than requiring; they suggest, they offer. The Contagious Leader knows how to communicate with each player to maximize his or her performance. Finally, as a player, Contagious Leaders must be willing to also do what they are asking of the other players. This process can get very complicated, especially for a hard-core Contained Leader who is attempting to move up to Contagious by practicing the same old, outdated habits of telling, demanding and dictating.

Asking Permission

Even the Contagious Leader will periodically assume too much, like the fact that an employee wants to be mentored in order to advance to the next level. Unfortunately, such an assumption can produce horrible results. First of all, the leader could take a great deal of valuable time mentoring someone who doesn't want to be mentored. In addition to the cost of the time, the leader ends up really annoying the person they have singled out for mentoring. Allow me to put this in very simple terms.

Growing up, our daughters Kate and Megan were fond of borrowing clothes from Beverly and me. Beverly's clothes were "wicked cool." Mine were just "wicked big," a fact that must have made them "wicked cool" as well, because they were highly sought after by our daughters. We'd get so infuriated when the girls would just go into our closets and take whatever they wanted. We would tell them, "If you'd just ask, you could probably borrow whatever you wanted." The same is true with mentoring. The key is to ask, and it is necessary for several reasons:

• As I said earlier, not every person wants to advance to the next level. Even if they did, they might not want your help, or they might not want your help at this very moment. Seeking permission in advance clarifies the situation. The other person knows you are the mentor, they have willingly accepted your offer for mentoring, and you know your time will not be wasted. I can't stress the importance of this enough. Even if you don't have an ongoing mentoring program but just want to offer a suggestion to an employee on how or why to do X, Y or Z, it is best to ask if they are open to "a suggestion" or to "some mentoring" before giving it. This is Psychology 101.

• Not asking is also just plain rude and intrusive, and no one likes to be intruded on. As I mentioned earlier, 96% of all change is forced and only 4% is initiated. It seems pretty obvious that the reason we don't initiate more change is because we have a hate relationship with change. We hate change because it has been forced on us so often. If we force mentoring, it will be received in much the same manner.

• We all prefer being given a choice. In this case, the choice is to accept or reject the "suggestion" or "mentoring." Something very powerful happens when we accept something after considering the choices. There is seriousness about the commitment. We find it true with our own coaching clients, many of whom come from organizations that have first engaged me for speaking programs. Often the organization will also ask me to assist their managers or Contained Leaders in developing Contagious Leadership habits and qualities. When the company is paying, it is sometimes difficult for the manager or Contained Leader to say, "No thank you." When they are given a genuine choice, however, those who accept take the coaching more seriously, prepare for each coaching session more rigorously, and will inevitably get more from the process. Please make sure that when you offer the choice, you are prepared to allow the other person to say no thanks. Beverly and I practice this frequently between us. One or the other of us will ask, "Are you open to some coaching on (this matter)?" On occasion, the other person will say, "No, not right now, but thanks!" Be prepared for this answer and allow it.

Otherwise, you won't be seeking permission at all.

• It is just more polite to ask. We have gotten away from being polite in business. Our manners have become horrendous. Asking for permission will lighten up your organization in ways you never thought possible.

Taking on Permission Mentoring

The steps to permission mentoring are really quite simple:

Step 1. Ask permission.
We have covered that pretty well.

Step 2. Establish parameters.
It is crucial to predetermine and agree to the boundaries of your mentoring. If your efforts will focus on the employee's becoming a Contagious Leader, you'll want to concentrate on developing the habits outlined in this book. Define each habit as we have, but also come to an agreement on your expectations. Have the employee do a self-assessment on each of the habits and compare it to your assessment before you begin the mentoring program. Come to some agreement as to the progress you and the person being mentored would like to see during the program. We also suggest that you set time limits for the program as a whole, as well as for each mentoring session. In our experience, ongoing programs, the week-in/week-out variety tend to run out of gas unless you are very good at mentoring and the person being mentored is very dedicated. Therefore, we suggest you clarify your time frame up front. For example, there was a time when I offered executive coaching on an ongoing basis. Every client would choose dates for two or three coaching calls per month and I would arrange my month accordingly. Someone in my office would hit the client's credit card once a month and I would proceed to do the calls. I noticed that, after a month or so, there was a sameness about the coaching calls, and the person I was

coaching would lose interest and/or arrive at coaching sessions unprepared.

The solution involved several aspects. First, I began to take fewer clients at one time. Second, each program is now focused for a maximum of 90 days and centers around one goal. Finally, I now require every client to pay for the entire 90 days in advance. This has the effect of making the client more committed. Regular monthly billing or debiting a credit card once a month can become routine and overlooked after a while. One large, up-front fee can get the client's attention right away and focus them on achieving the most value for their time and money.

Since most of you will be mentoring people internally, you won't have these billing considerations to contend with. You may still wish to consider using the principles, however. Part of establishing parameters is to outline what you expect in terms of performance as well as results. You need to find a way to tell the people you are mentoring that you expect them to take this seriously and keep their commitments. When they say they are going to do something, you expect them to do it. You may also want to consider some consequences of their failure to meet their commitments and recognition of commitments met. I once had a coach who had the right to call me, any hour of the day or night, if I failed to check in with her by 10 PM every evening. Even if I called in to inform her that I had botched the whole day and did not keep a single commitment, it was better than not calling at all. Together we set-up the parameters — what was expected and what would happen if expectations were not met.

Let me offer one final caveat about establishing parameters. It is best to keep the parameters focused on activities or behaviors rather than results. There are so many variables outside an individual's control that can impact results. Coming to agreement about the desired outcome is certainly important because it keeps the coach and the coachee focused. As Dr. Stephen Covey said, it forces both parties to "begin with the end in mind." However, your mentoring should largely focus on the activities and behaviors that will move the individual in the direction of the desired outcome. Let's consider an example:

You have been asked to mentor someone in sales and you agree that by the end of 90 days they will close X new accounts. That is the "what" and it is very important. Your mentoring, however, is best directed at the "how," the activities and behaviors that the individual needs to improve to accomplish the goal. It is entirely possible that you could have a highly effective mentoring program even though the individual does not close the desired number of new accounts, because you will be measuring his or her progress on the activities and behaviors necessary to achieve that goal. Now, if the person consistently misses the goal, you will both need to look at the appropriateness of the activities and behaviors that were established to meet the goal.

Step 3. Set aside uninterrupted time.

Although you will want this process to be as active and fluid as possible, setting aside uninterrupted regular time for discussion, review, measurement and feedback is essential. It is critical that this time be exclusively devoted to the mentoring program. Do not relegate your mentoring review to the last 15 minutes of your biweekly status meeting. It dishonors the process, diminishes the importance of your program, and spotlights, in a very public way, your lack of commitment to being a Contagious Leader and developing other Contagious Leaders.

We have found that a mentoring session once or twice a month with each person is a terrific way to begin the program. Although some of the participants may want a weekly session, we have found this to be too frequent. Be careful, however. The more time between reviews, the easier it is to not pay attention to the process. You may find that you need to remind yourself to keep the process active and fluid by putting notes in your calendar to send a note or email or call the person you are coaching and check in.

These activities will keep you in the permission mentoring con-versation. The worst thing you can do is allow the other person to feel forgotten.

Step 4. Use involved recognition.

It has been said many times that the best way to learn anything is to teach it. The permission mentoring process is a great way for you to also practice the habits and qualities of a Contagious Leader. For example, your attitude will be very impor-tant, you'll want to focus on the strengths of the individual, and you'll use involved recognition as often as possible. Be on the lookout for opportunities to recognize the person you are mentor-ing for their actions and behavior. Recognizing even the smallest behavior with as much detail as possible will help the person build confidence in their ability to be a Contagious Leader, while learning to use involved recognition themselves. Also, a very important part of this mentoring process is modeling. If you rip them to pieces for every little thing they don't do as well as you would like and miss opportunities to publicly acknowledge the great things they have done, they will model the very same behavior. Permission mentoring is a great way to keep you on track as a Contagious Leader.

Step 5. Measure, measure, measure.

The job of a quarterback in football is to move the ball up the field. The team can't score points unless the quarterback does this. As a Contagious Leader, you are like the quarterback. Your job is to make sure the team as a whole, and each player, keeps moving in the right direction. A part of that goal is to develop future Contagious Leaders, not just one who will replace you when you get your big promotion to corporate vice president. That's Contained Leadership thinking! The Contagious Leader will have several individuals in the Contagious Leadership pipeline. It is important to keep track of how each person is doing and how many you have at any given stage of development. Let me give you an example:

Let's say you have determined that, for a person to be promoted from a manager to a director, they need to have developed all the habits of a Contagious Leader (including the 13 character qualities) to a level of 8 or better on the 10-point self-assessment scale. Further, let's assume that the final score is an average of the self-assessment, your assessment and a 360° feedback from at least one person reporting directly to that person. You'll want to know at any given point how many individuals you have in the permission mentoring program at a 6, 7, 8, 9 or 10. The 8-10 candidates are Contagious Leaders, the 5-7s are Contagious Leader in Progress, and those in the under-5 category are Beginning Contagious Leaders. After your permission mentoring program has been operational for a while, you will be able to tell not only how many are in each category but in what time frame individuals are expected to move from one to another. You will be able to look through a Permission Mentoring File on any person in your organization and anticipate that they will be an 8 or better, and therefore ready both for promotion and to begin mentoring others by a certain date. Your own performance and promotability will be measured on how many individuals you have in each category relative to the goals you agreed to at the beginning of the year.

Every organization and every Contagious Leader will have their own system for incorporating the Contagious Leadership permission mentoring system into their culture. The critical thing is that it be incorporated and measured on a regular basis with incentives built into the system.

The Benefits of Permission Mentoring

A permission mentoring program can focus individuals, departments, regions and even your entire organization. Initiating such an effort trumpets the Contagious Leader's intentions about the way the organization will be managed. Done properly, as outlined, it declares your commitment to Contagious Leadership and signals your intention to involve and impact the entire culture. This focus begins to be modeled immediately. It brings individuals and departments together in a common objective of creating Contagious Leadership.

Chapter 11

Getting Started

Creating Contagious Leadership

An environment of Contagious Leadership can be more fun and produce more results than you ever thought possible. Just imagine arriving at your job every day knowing that you would be surrounded with energy, excitement, commitment and individuals who are totally dedicated to the habits of Contagious Leadership. Imagine, if your business were that much fun, the results that you and your team would produce. Imagine how much attrition might be reduced, how much easier it might be to attract really great people, and how much more fulfilled each person on your team might feel at the end of the day.

If you think this is pie-in-the-sky thinking, I challenge you to prove yourself right. Go ahead! You see, in order to prove yourself right, you must first prove that Contagious Leadership will not produce the benefits we have offered throughout this book. To accomplish this goal, you have to first give it a try. Think carefully before you agree because, once started, you'll find it hard to go back to the old ways of the Contained Leader. If you don't think so, just ask any of the top people at GE where it would be today had it not taken on its Contagious Leadership initiative.

Ok, so are you in? Are you willing to give it an honest try? Great, let's get started.

Like so many of the other areas of Contagious Leadership, there is a logical sequencing of commitments and behaviors that will make your efforts a success:

Step 1. Be a Contagious Leader.

Did you really think I was going to let you write some memo announcing the company's latest greatest program for improving results and leave it at that? You didn't think I was going to let you off the hook that easy did you? Oh, no! The first step is to be a Contagious Leader yourself. You have to model it. Developing Contagious Leadership requires two decisions before anything can happen. First, you have to decide that leadership, not management, is your top priority. You will continue to value every person on your team at every level — worker, manager, Contained Leader and Contagious Leader. Your priority, however, will be to develop Contagious Leaders and thereby paint your culture with the 9 Habits of Contagious Leaders. In so doing, you will make your second decision: to walk the walk and talk the talk of a Contagious Leader and be measured by the criteria outlined in this book — the same criteria for measuring every other person on your team.

Plain and simple, double standards will guarantee that your Contagious Leadership initiative never gets off the ground. If that is your goal, then by all means say one thing and do another. If, on the other hand, you are truly dedicated to creating a contagious culture, you must be that culture. Mahatma Gandhi once said, "You must be the change you wish to see in the world."

What a concept! Walk it, talk it, be it, be passionate about it, model it, and it will happen.

Making this decision does not mean that you hold workers, managers or Contained Leaders in contempt. Remember, the Contagious Leader looks to people's greatness at every level. We all have a role to play on the team and every team will need workers, managers, Contained Leaders and Contagious Leaders. Since this latter category is in such short supply, you'll be recruiting and training for this group while maintaining a healthy respect for the contribution of every person.

Step 2. Establish the high bar.

Every culture, every company and every individual is different. The beauty of this Contagious Leadership program is that you "get to" make decisions early on in the game that reflect your company. I am not suggesting that you make some sweeping generalizations and apply them to your company/department. Rather, appropriately apply some principles within your organization. These standards are your choice. It is your company or department, and you get to create whatever culture you want. Be careful not to wimp out on us though. Sometimes it is easy to set the high bar too low.

For each habit and each quality for which you get to decide the standard, there is a high point at which you will say, "This person, relative to this habit, is a Contagious Leader in my organization." If you work in a bank accounting department, you might think it a bit inappropriate to set your "risk" high bar at 10. Perhaps you want people to strive for 7 with regard to risk just to make sure they aren't getting stuck in the "what-has-been box." On the other hand, given that you grew up in the accounting department of the very same bank, it may be easy for you to set a standard for spotlighting way too low at 4, reflecting your own natural discomfort with giving and getting recognition. Avoid this natural tendency. In fact, it is a good idea to have more people involved in establishing the high bar. Consider involving the top people on your team, but keep the number below 10 because beyond that point it may get a bit unwieldy. Have each person offer their own estimate of the standard for each habit and quality, and then have them rank the relative importance of each.

The bottom line is that each Contagious Leader, each company, each department has the ability to determine its own leadership standards so it can measure how well it is doing. Remember I said earlier that when I do speaking engagements, I ask the audience if they believe character is important? More often than not, they all agree it is important but they are not at all sure how to define it. The same is true for measuring the habits and qualities of a Contagious Leader. Unless we set the standards and then measure performance, how will we ever know how well we are doing?

Step 3. Build endorsement.

Don't be surprised if, at first, the people around you are a bit nervous and skeptical. We generally don't like change, and we certainly don't like it forced on us. Building endorsement requires us to be sensitive to these attitudes and implement our program so that it encourages, not discourages, participation. When GE launched the Work-Out program, where workers, managers and leaders came together to share ideas and break down barriers, it was voluntary at first. It was rather like a town meeting. Many of the workers and managers attended with healthy skepticism. Before they would participate actively and willingly, they needed to know that it was a safe environment and that they could speak without any risk that their comments would be held against them. In addition, they needed to know that if they offered an idea, someone would actually respond to it. So Jack Welch and those who put the program together created some strategies to build endorsement. First, everyone was asked to wear khakis and t-shirts to the Work-Out sessions, thereby making it difficult to distinguish a worker from a manager or leader. Furthermore, the leaders were instructed to respond to ideas, on the spot, in one of three ways: approve it, reject it, or ask for more information.

It didn't take long for everyone to realize that this effort was serious. Later, after some of the walls came down, it was actually possible to *require* attendance at these sessions.

Building endorsement takes time and genuine effort. This is where double standards will kill a program. Here are a few strategies for building endorsement:

- Set goals and make sure every person on your team knows exactly what you are up to, why, and what you hope to accomplish.

- Implement a vibrant communication program (early, often and congruently) and make sure everyone knows:
  - What you are doing
  - Who is doing it
  - Why you are doing it
  - How well you are doing
  - Who is doing well

- Make sure the communication is internal and external
- Remember to focus on successes.

Step 4. Keep score.

This is perhaps the most important step of all. We all have a tendency to start and stop programs. They are great ideas at the time and then life shows up and the "really important things" take precedence. You can't allow this to happen. Keeping score is a matter of discipline and focus. It is implementation, the key to any long-term success. I suggest that you automate as much of the scorekeeping as possible. Make the self-evaluation form (page 116) an integral part of your performance review system. Every time reviews are scheduled, make sure that the employee, the manager and at least one person reporting directly to the person being reviewed completes and signs the self-evaluation form. Calculate the average scores and chart the progress. It takes discipline, but it will pay huge dividends in the future.

The two most important areas here are frequency and specificity. Your performance reviews, especially when you are getting started, may need to be more frequent, at least for the first two quarters. I would like to see them completed monthly if for no other reason than to communicate your commitment to the program.

Step 5. Celebrate success.

Here is your big chance to model Contagious Leadership. There are a number of specific strategies you'll need to implement in your spotlighting and involved recognition programs.

- **Be public.** Spotlighting can be effective in any environment but, done in a public way, it will have an enormous impact and more lasting value.
- **Be immediate**. To the employee, there is nothing more important than celebrating their success. The sooner you honor their accomplishments, the more impact it will have

on them and the rest of the organization. Conversely, the longer you wait, the more the employee will realize that you are just providing lip service to spotlighting, involved recognition and vibrant communication.

- **Be specific**. "Good job, Harry" barely works. Much better: "You did a great job handling those customers, Harry. They felt listened to and are now more committed than ever to our customer-service program. Building loyal customers like this makes us unstoppable. Thanks for the great job!"

- **Focus on strengths**. If your goal is to deflate the balloon, go ahead and spend your day pointing out what hasn't been done. If, on the other hand, you are really committed to excellence, focus on the excellent things that people do.

- **Communicate accomplishments**.

  Celebrate often.

  Be sure to celebrate the 9 habits and 13 qualities rather than always just the numbers.

    — Send handwritten "Way-to-Go!" note cards as often as possible. Celebrate even the smallest success. And be sure to enroll all the "higher-ups" in the process. You just can't measure the impact of someone's receiving a handwritten note at home from the CEO thanking them for a job well done. It takes no time for the grapevine to spread that luscious piece of news.

    Try this. Sit down right now and write five handwritten "Way-to-Go!" notes on your stationery to people on your team. Handwrite the envelope as well. It may take you all of ten minutes. In your note, tell each person why you appreciate them. Be as specific as possible, telling them what you appreciate them for. And then write five more next week, one a day. The week after that, write two each day. See what happens and how much things change. Even if you don't get any feedback at all, I promise you'll feel and notice a difference. You might even suggest that all your direct reports take on the same assignment. Imagine people arriving home one evening to find a note from you or one of the other Contagious Leaders on your team. How do you think they'll feel?

— Have your team vote on the Contagious Leader of the month. They get to attend a Contagious Leadership luncheon with the CEO.

— Put up a Contagious Leadership Wall of Fame — pictures of Contagious Leaders with a caption detailing the specifics that distinguishes each person. Display it prominently in the lobby or the lunch room.

These are just some suggestions. There are limitless ways to celebrate your Contagious Leaders and your Contagious Leadership program. Bring your team together for a one-hour brainstorming session to think of more. It will be fun and highly productive.

Step 6. Cultivate the culture.

Cultivating a Contagious Leadership culture requires us to be ever mindful of the barriers to that culture. We have to remove the disincentives to the behaviors of Contagious Leaders. Consider these strategies:

• **Stop celebrating the wrong behaviors**. Joe — the guy in finance with the behavioral style of a switchblade, the one who only cares about the bottom line, the guy who is on his fourth marriage because he works 90 hours a week and expects everyone else to do the same — is promoted to executive vice president. How often have we seen this movie? What is being celebrated here, the "what" or the "how"? Contagious Leadership or ruthless Contained Leadership? Contagious Leaders are congruent, all the time, in every decision.

• **Make it OK to be a Contagious Leader**. Creating Contagious Leaders takes a commitment to doing just that. Whatever your feelings about GE, its track record for developing leaders and delivering results is indisputable. How did this happen? Jack Welch decided it would be so, and he made it OK to be a leader, not just a manager.

• **Be personally involved in the process**. You can't delegate a Contagious Leadership initiative, you have to be involved in the process. For it to be effective, you have to be a Contagious Leader, reward Contagious Leadership, and teach others to be Contagious Leaders. It may not be all you do, but you have to be involved in the process. It is important to be very clear on this one point. We are talking about a cultural shift for most companies. Some people say, "Change is like moving the Queen Mary; it happens slowly." Does it really have to be so slow? My guess is the changes at GE would have taken much longer had someone other than Welch been in charge. He understood that leadership is not hands-off, management is.

• **Appoint a CLO (Contagious Leadership Officer)**. Give a person a big title, big office, big bucks and lots of authority to implement, keep score and celebrate success.

Ready, Set, Hold It!

Are you sure about setting up a Contagious Leadership environment? It sounds great, but what a big step! What if it doesn't work, what if you look like an idiot, what will your boss think?

Slow down! Relax! This isn't nuclear warfare and no one is going to get captured and tortured by aliens. All we have been talking about is creating a more enjoyable and rewarding culture, where individuals are recognized frequently for the many, many, many good things they do and for their strengths, not their weaknesses. Moreover, respect is shown for each individual by the way we communicate with them (early, often and congruently); reward the "how," not just the "what"; hold character in high regard; and recognize that the success of our company and everyone in it depends on our ability to develop and nurture leaders instead of more managers pushing papers and people. In the next chapter I have outlined a few ways that others have accomplished this cultural shift.

The worst thing that will happen, as long as you are truly genuine in your commitments, is that people will feel more respected, more valued, more appreciated. In turn, they will be more focused on a team program, more willing to contribute to others, more sincere about their commitments, more determined to fulfill what they set out to do. They will have better attitudes by being more authentic and will spend less time waiting for someone or something to inspire them. Their motivation will come from within. The net result is that the team will be like the scullers I used to watch along the Charles River in Boston every morning, rowing in unison, pulling together, exerting the right amount of energy in the right place at exactly the right time.

Who knows, your organization might even become rich with leaders — Contagious Leaders who develop and nurture more leaders by recognizing and rewarding the qualities that set leaders apart. The process may even spread as everyone from the mailroom to the boardroom catches the Contagious Leadership fever.

Environments of Contagious Leadership do not just happen.
They start with a decision;
the individual decides to be a Contagious Leader
and the company decides to create
a culture of Contagious Leaders.

Figure 1 — Establishing the High Bar

For each of the Creating Contagious Leadership qualities and habits, rate yourself on a scale of 1-10 with 10 being perfect. For example, a 10 rating for "attitude" means you always have a "can do" attitude. Be honest now! Then rank each quality and habit to determine areas needing your attention.

Habit/Quality	Rating	Ranking
Spotlighting	_____	_____
Cultivating character	_____	_____
Attitude	_____	_____
Authenticity	_____	_____
Contribution	_____	_____
Commitment	_____	_____
Determination	_____	_____
Discipline	_____	_____
Drive	_____	_____
Embracing change	_____	_____
Focus	_____	_____
Integrity	_____	_____
Motivation	_____	_____
Creating possibility	_____	_____
Risk	_____	_____
Involved recognition	_____	_____
Looking to greatness	_____	_____
Vibrant communication	_____	_____
Unobstructed vision	_____	_____
Touching lives	_____	_____
A passionate stand	_____	_____
Permission mentoring	_____	_____
Total score	_____	_____

Chapter 12

Contagious Leaders in Action

Cultivating Character

It was 1980 and I had joined the advertising agency of Humphrey Browning MacDougall (HBM) only a few months earlier. It was a totally different experience for me. Having come out of the banking business, I was accustomed to a quiet, rather unemotional work environment. HBM was anything but unemotional.

Ed Eskandarian had hired me as an account executive. It took a lot of nerve to do that, since I had been vice president of marketing for one of the agency's clients. Ed and the president of the bank made an arrangement. HBM could hire me as long as I did not work on the other banking account at the agency, the Bank of Boston. It was fine by me.

Within a very short time of my joining HBM, we began to hear rumors that the Bank of Boston account was in trouble. Where there is smoke, there is usually fire, so within a few weeks the agency was told there would be a review. In the agency business, the term "review" usually means the agency has lost the business but the client doesn't have the heart or decency to say so. Participating in a review can be like dying a slow death, at least to everyone but Ed Eskandarian. He has one of those remarkable attitudes about life and business. To Ed, "review" means a second chance, an opportunity to prove how terrific the agency really is. So we were in this review and the pressure began to mount. A large "pitch team" was assembled and they worked day and night preparing for the opportunity to present new, fresh work. Sometime later, the other agencies in the review were announced. The schedule was also announced, and HBM was to present last, at eight in the morning.

The story got very interesting as the date of the presentation approached. *The Boston Globe* began to run a series of articles about a particular underworld figure and hinted of ties with the Bank of Boston. By the day of the presentation, the agency had been working night and day for several months and, although everyone felt great about the work, two things were obvious. First, everyone was exhausted, and second, we were all concerned about the review and whether it was just delaying the inevitable. No one said it out loud but it was a concern.

At 8:00 on the morning of the pitch, the team assembled in the board room of the Bank of Boston. There were long faces everywhere. That morning *The Boston Globe* had run a huge front-page headline story about the alleged connection between the bank and the underworld. The bank, out of courtesy, allowed us to make the presentation, even though they probably were not as attentive as they might have otherwise been. Ed closed the presentation and was brilliant. He told the bank that advertising was the least of their concerns and they should probably not invest in any media programs over the next few months. If they wanted some public relations guidance, we would make ourselves available in any way that would best serve the bank. He took a passionate stand for the Bank of Boston's greatness.

The Bank of Boston was a large and important account for HBM. Nevertheless, Ed Eskandarian put aside what the agency needed and wanted and concerned himself with what was right. Over the years, I have thought about this often as a great example of character. In an industry not known for character or its concern for others, it was nice to know that at least one person was concerned about the "how" as well as the "what." Ed Eskandarian believed in cultivating character and modeled it every day. It was an honor to work with him.

Touching Lives

Marc Williams is a well-educated, thoughtful, articulate man. If you met him on the street or over the telephone, you might be surprised to learn that he is also a bobcat driver in Arizona. He moves dirt around for a living. Your impression might be that he is too articulate for a bobcat driver. But Marc Williams is not like most people. If he were like most of us, he would show up in the morning, move some dirt, take a coffee break, move more dirt, have lunch, move a little more dirt, take another break, move some dirt, and go home to have dinner and watch some TV before getting up the next day to do it all over again.

Not Marc Williams! His passion is creating things from dirt. Beverly calls him a "dirt architect." He does amazing things with that bobcat and dirt. He creates landscapes that make a difference to people and improves the quality of their lives. He gets in that bobcat, and all day long he studies the landscape, moves the dirt, studies and moves, shapes the ground, moves the dirt. He loves his work and it shows. Marc Williams has a passion for making a difference. He touches lives.

Unobstructed Vision

A few years ago, Beverly and I attended a program put on by the Enterprise Network, a great organization. The featured speaker was Steve Hanson, then president of ON Semiconductor. ON Semiconductor had once been a division of Motorola and Steve had been president of the division. Steve's presentation that evening was not about Motorola or ON Semiconductor so much as it was about having the vision to alter a company culture. At the time, ON was experiencing some pretty terrific success, and Steve said it was largely a function of culture.

Toward the end of Steve's presentation, an audience member asked what Steve had learned during his business transitions. Steve had risen from entry-level engineer to product manager to a stint in Scotland to division vice president to corporate vice president to division president in the span of 28 years with a Fortune 500 company. He answered that he had learned more and had more fun during the past 18 months than during his previous 28 years combined. His answer was not intended to reflect negatively on his previous employer, but rather to comment on the effects of the culture in his new organization. You see, as soon the decision was made to spin the division off and attempt an IPO, Steve and others knew the culture would have to change. They would have to operate as a startup, not a division of one of the largest companies in the world. They would have to create a "focused, fun, fast" culture and they would have to do it quickly.

Steve Hanson knew there was only one way to make this change. He and the others on his management team would have to "be the change they wished to see." They would all have to be Contagious Leaders. Furthermore, they would have to cause the changes in people who had spent the better part of their working lives with the prior division of the Fortune 500 company. They had unobstructed vision and implemented a vibrant communications program so that everyone knew exactly what the company was, where they were headed, and what was expected of each person. Finally, Steve and the others on the management team actually conducted the training. They did this for two reasons. First, they were no longer a division of a Fortune 500 company with unlimited resources and they chose to do the training themselves rather than hire outside providers. More importantly, they knew that no outsider could articulate their unobstructed vision as well as they could. This training began long before the actual spin-off of the division.

The result was astounding. Several thousand employees appeared to seamlessly move from one culture to another overnight. It seemed as though they were employees of the Fortune 500 giant on Friday, and on Monday they were part of a "focused, fun, fast" start up. Sounds like several thousand employees caught the Contagious Leadership fever.

Determination, Commitment and Self Motivation

Allow a very proud father to share an amazing story about determination, commitment and self-motivation. Megan Hersey is 20 and has just recently completed her studies to be a world-class hairdresser, something she has shown passion for since she was very little. She is excited about her new career. There was a time, however, when, deep down inside, she wondered, and we wondered, if she would ever finish high school.

Megan was never all that interested in school. It was OK, but not something that inspired her. Oh, heck, let's be honest here. She hated school, always did and probably always will. With each passing year, however, she seemed to have more of a challenge. She was tested for what seemed like everything in an effort to help her. Like so many other kids of this generation, she was diagnosed with ADD and prescribed Ritalin, which never did seem to do much for her. She graduated from middle school and went on to a private high school. It was a very difficult year. Academically, she had challenges that seemed to frustrate her more and more. Toward the end of that year, she was tested again, and this time it was determined that she had a form of dyslexia. Her frustration was very high, her self-esteem low and worsening. She was held back as a freshman, a huge blow to her self-esteem. Making matters worse, the school announced that they were not equipped to accommodate her needs. When the public high school laid out a plan for helping Megan, she enrolled. Unfortunately, the high school never quite got it together. Megan, more frustrated than ever, worked hard, but couldn't quite make it happen. It looked like she would be held back a second time.

We have all heard the story of the sow's ear having a silver lining. Megan, through a series of events, was able to enroll in the Landmark School, an extraordinary place with great people and a wonderful understanding of what Megan needed. Unfortunately, she had to enroll as a boarding student. Although the school was only 30 minutes from home, in her mind she had to leave her family and friends. It was disappointing at best and further demoralizing. But she took it like a trooper. Her first year as a sophomore was a year of adjustment, structure and discipline. Megan had to earn even the most seemingly insignificant reward. It took a bit of getting used to, but she hung in there once again. In her junior year, things began to worsen again. In the Fall, Megan just wasn't herself. She had bouts of frustration, sadness and anger. Tested once again, Megan learned of a chemical challenge that required medication. This was not great news for such a fragile self-esteem. Nonetheless, Megan once again stood strong. This funny, beautiful, creative and compassionate girl could have given up any number of times, could have just thrown in the towel, and could have quit trying, but she never did.

Her senior year was relatively smooth sailing. We attended her graduation and she was beaming. Megan knew she had a lot to be proud of. Somehow, down deep, she knew all along that the choice was hers. Somehow she found the strength to continue, to look her challenges square in the face every day and boldly declare, "Come ahead! You can knock me down, but I'll keep getting up. This is my life and you are not in charge!"

It may take years for Megan to fully appreciate just what she accomplished. Her determination, commitment and level of self-motivation far surpassed what we have come to reasonably expect from kids. Today, she is a beautiful, beaming, 20-year-old woman embarking on a new career. Every day she looks the world squarely in the face and boldly declares, "Is that all you've got?"

Integrity

I was the keynote speaker at the annual sales meeting of Data Systems International (DSI) in January 2001. Mike McGraw and I met for the first time during dinner just before my talk. We discussed my theme, "The Character of a Winner," and eventually got around to the subject of integrity. Then Mike told me a great story.

It seems that one of DSI's clients had mistakenly double-paid them. At the time, DSI sold hardware, software and service solutions to a variety of manufacturing companies, so the typical invoice was no small amount. When Mike said the client had double-paid, his eyes lit up to punctuate the point that we were talking about some serious money. Nearly two months after learning about this situation, a person in the finance department went to Mike to inform him of the situation and, in Mike's words, "see how he wanted it handled." The finance person told Mike that several executives and supervisors had met on a number of occasions to discuss the situation but had not come to a conclusion about the best way to resolve it. The client was still unaware of the double payment and it was time for Mike's input.

Mike McGraw listened to the story carefully, all the while trying not to explode. When the finance person was finished with the presentation, Mike simply said, "I think you know what I would like you to do. Go back to your office and come back tomorrow and just tell me what would be the right thing to do."

To Mike McGraw, doing the right thing is what integrity, character and Contagious Leadership is all about.

Involved Recognition

When we first moved to Arizona from Boston, Don Henninger was the editor of *The Business Journal of Phoenix* and Joelle Hadley was the publisher. I had gotten to know Don but only recently met Joelle. When Joelle made a major life and career decision to leave the *Journal* and start her own training company, Don was the likely candidate to move into her position. He did, and in August 2001, he wrote this editorial about Joelle. It is a fabulous example of practicing involved recognition, spotlighting and vibrant communication.

The Business Journal of Phoenix — August 13, 2001
OPINION
From the Publisher
In recognition of a friend, former boss
Don Henninger

Every year when we publish our list of the most influential business and community leaders in Arizona, we make a point to leave one key person off the roster.

When we run our list of 40 up-and-comers under

40 years old, we still do not allow that name to make the cut.

And last year when we ran our section honoring the accomplishments of Valley businesswomen, we kept her out of that game, too.

It's not because she didn't deserve to be included or there was a conspiracy against her. Hardly. Fact is, she would have been a slam-dunk to be a player on all those lists.

No, Joelle Hadley's position as publisher of The Business Journal *automatically knocked her out of any consideration to be covered in such a way in our paper. Came with the job. Anyone who understands newspaper credibility issues would find that logic easy to follow.*

But Hadley now has spent her last day as publisher. She left the paper to launch a new career and begin her own business. So today, it is appropriate to offer a little make-up.

Fact is, Hadley has been one of the Valley's most influential business and community leaders. In her six-year reign, she was active in a long list of community groups, including the Greater Phoenix Chamber of Commerce and Greater Phoenix Leadership. To describe her involvement in non-profit groups would take up far more room than this column will allow. Most passionate to her have been the American Cancer Society and Fresh Start Women's Foundation.

Fact is, she should be on the list of 40 under-40 up-and-comers. For much of her tenure here, she could have qualified for under 30. She was named ad director when she was 24 and publisher at 28. Those achievements speak for themselves.

Fact is, her accomplishments would land her on

anyone's list of the top businesswomen, too. Evidence: Her success at the paper combined with her passion and advocacy in recognizing the achievements of other women.

Hadley's people skills were strong enough and sincere enough to pierce through even the thickest skin of a skeptical editor. Her people-focused values were always a core part of the way she ran her business and the way she lives her life. She was true to herself and true to her co-workers.

Hadley will be a tough act to follow as I take her chair in the publisher's office. But I have one thing going for me. I had a great teacher.

© 2001 American City Business Journals Inc. Reprinted with permission from Don Henninger, Publisher, *The Phoenix Business Journal*

Examples of Contagious Leaders are everywhere. I invite you to share your stories by emailing me at *stories@creating contagiousleadership.com*. We will post them to the website, under your name if you wish or anonymously if that suits you. The point here is that we can all learn from sharing each other's experiences.

As I mentioned at the very beginning of this book, Contagious Leadership has nothing to do with title, background, education or position. We all have the ability to be Contagious Leaders at home, in our communities, churches, schools and, yes, in our jobs. Think for just a minute what the world would be like if each of us practiced cultivating character and modeled the habits outlined in this book. It just might be that Contagious Leadership would spread and the world would be a better place for us all.

About the Author

When it comes to business and leadership, John Hersey has "walked the walk." He knows about leadership because that is exactly what he has done throughout his 30-year career: lead organizations and teams.

He was vice president of marketing for a $1 billion bank at the age of 28, senior vice president for one of the largest advertising agencies in the country and founder of three successful companies (one went public and one went international) by the time he was 40. He and his partner and wife, Beverly Belury, live in Arizona where they pursue their passion for helping individuals and organizations create Contagious Leadership.

John Hersey helps companies hire, develop, inspire and retain the individuals necessary to Create Contagious Leadership. He speaks to audiences at dozens of conventions, national and regional sales meetings and executive conferences each year and conducts workshops to assist leaders in the implementation of the principles and concepts presented in *Creating Contagious Leadership*. Many of his clients see him as a trusted partner and executive advisor in the process of transforming their organizations to meet the leadership challenges of the next decade. To help your organization Create Contagious Leadership, contact John at:

John Hersey International
Creating Contagious Leadership
PO Box 17029
Fountain Hills, Arizona 85269
Phone: 480-836-7474
Fax: 480-816-3469
E-mail: Beverly@Johnhersey.com
Website: www.Johnhersey.com